PREVENTING
Long-Term ELs

Transforming Schools
to Meet Core Standards

Margarita Espino Calderón
Liliana Minaya-Rowe

CORWIN
A SAGE Company

For information:

Corwin
A SAGE Company
2455 Teller Road
Thousand Oaks, California 91320
www.corwin.com

SAGE Ltd.
1 Oliver's Yard
55 City Road
London EC1Y 1SP
United Kingdom

SAGE Pvt. Ltd.
B 1/I 1 Mohan Cooperative
   Industrial Area
Mathura Road, New Delhi 110 044
India

SAGE Asia-Pacific Pte. Ltd.
33 Pekin Street #02-01
Far East Square
Singapore 048763

Printed in the United States of America

Library of Congress Cataloging-in-Publication Data

Calderón, Margarita.
Preventing long-term ELs : transforming schools to meet core standards / Margarita Espino Calderón, Liliana Minaya-Rowe.
     p. cm.
Includes bibliographical references and index.
ISBN 978-1-4129-7416-5 (pbk.)
   1. Education, Bilingual—United States. 2. School improvement programs—United States. 3. Second language acquisition—United States. I. Minaya-Rowe, Liliana. II. Title.

LC3731.C294 2011
428.2'4—dc22   2010037118

This book is printed on acid-free paper.

11   12   13   14   10 9 8 7 6 5 4 3 2

Acquisitions Editor:	Dan Alpert
Associate Editor:	Megan Bedell
Editorial Assistant:	Sarah Bartlett
Production Editor:	Veronica Stapleton
Copy Editor:	Tina Hardy
Typesetter:	C&M Digitals (P) Ltd.
Proofreader:	Dennis W. Webb
Indexer:	Molly Hall
Cover Designer:	Karine Hovsepian
Permissions Editor:	Karen Ehrmann

Contents

Prologue

Conclusions from committees and panels on teacher education, language-minority children, and general reading and writing instruction coincide on the fact that effective teaching is the dominant factor in student learning (August & Shanahan, 2006, 2008; National Research Council, 2010; Short & Fitzsimmons, 2007). Concomitantly, other research shows that there are certain school structures that enable effective teaching (Calderón & Slavin, 2010; Fullan, 2010; School Leadership for the 21st Century Initiative, 2000; Sergiovanni, 2007). Effective instruction is nested in effective school structures. Success with English Learners (ELs) is nested in teacher success.

Each year the number of Long-Term English Learners (LT-ELs) in middle and high schools grows. In 2008 the approximate number was about 6,000,000, in 2009 about 8,000,000. These are students that have been in U. S. schools since kindergarten. As larger numbers of LT-ELs and struggling readers reach middle and high schools, all teachers are being impacted with the need to learn how to address these students' needs. Elementary teachers recognize that they need to provide more challenging meaningful instruction to ready the students for secondary schools. Mainstream content teachers in middle and high schools have seen how the large numbers of ELs are spilling out of English as a Second Language (ESL) or sheltered classrooms and into theirs and want to do what is right for all students. Therefore, the real need for most schools in the country today is to provide structures and support for teachers so they can move in these directions. Without better support for teachers, we can't expect better student outcomes.

There have been several longitudinal comprehensive studies that have shown how to simultaneously work on school structures, teacher support mechanisms, and effective instruction for ELs (August & Shanahan, 2008; Calderón, 2009; Calderón & Slavin, 2010; Lesaux et al., 2010; Slavin et al., in press). The randomized longitudinal study comparing student outcomes in

Spanish and English for students in transitional bilingual and structured English immersion programs identified 10 basic features that cut across programs, languages of instruction, and school contexts. The same features were applied and tested in the longitudinal study on adolescent ELs, *"Preparing Teachers of Math, Science, Social Studies and Language Arts to Teach Language, Literacy and Content"* (Calderón, Minaya-Rowe, Carreón, Durán, & Fitch, 2010). A midterm analysis of the instructional components of this study were published in an earlier Corwin book entitled, *Teaching Reading to English Language Learners, Grades 6–12* (Calderón, 2007).

The basic components or features that cut across language of instruction, school settings, and teacher and student background are as follows:

1. School structures

2. Instructional components

3. Equitable materials in first and second language (L1 and L2)

4. Professional development

5. Leadership

6. Parent/family support teams

7. Tutoring

8. Benchmark assessments

9. Coaching of teachers

10. Monitoring Implementation

The intent of this book is to provide the "tools for schools" to implement these features. Our objective is to help schools do the following:

> Apply more rigor into their integration of language, literacy, and subject domains
> Institute more comprehensive professional development programs that are also relevant to each grade level, subject domain, and state of teacher development
> Identify EL-focused performance or benchmark assessments
> Capture teacher and student growth and success
> Track effectiveness of school structures (e.g., teacher support, parental engagement, administrative effort, quality of professional development, and Teacher Learning Communities).

The 10 features are described throughout the book, gliding through various chapters. However, particular emphasis is given in the following chapters:

Chapter 1. U.S. Schools Failing ELs: A Call for Change: This chapter condenses the state of affairs, what we already know, and the moral and legal commitments we have from here on to meet the urgent instructional needs of LT-ELs. The chapter poses an empirically based theory of action in an age of core standards, globalization, and 21st-century skills to address the achievement gap of ELs so that they graduate.

Chapter 2. The ELs: This chapter describes the range of EL educational backgrounds and provides an exploratory profile that can help schools target the areas for assessment and the type of instructional intervention most appropriate to EL's and schools' needs. The chapter also informs a school's improvement planning to implement its own theory of change.

Chapter 3. Tools for Schools: The Framework for Preventing LT-ELs: The framework and tools discussed in this chapter focus on the 10 features and structures for quality instruction and effective schooling for ELs and school success. The chapter also sets the groundwork for the most basic feature: extensive professional development, which consists of intensive training, follow-up coaching, refresher workshops, and observation protocols to measure fidelity of implementation affecting student performance. If schools are to create meaningful change, well-prepared educators will make these changes materialize in the most compelling and operative way.

Chapter 4. Instructional Program Options for ELs: Some schools prefer and can implement different types of bilingual programs. Others might want to, but they are restricted by politics, shortage of bilingual teachers, too many different language groups, or finances. In either case, all programs can work for ELs and other students. This chapter discusses programs that provide for the language and academic development students need to succeed in school and be part of the global skills race. Program options are listed, along with their benefits and potential drawbacks.

Chapter 5. Selecting and Teaching Academic Vocabulary/Discourse: This is the first of five chapters dedicated to the description of what we mean by effective instruction for ELs. This chapter touches on the research on vocabulary and adds to this body of research from our recent empirical studies. It goes beyond "just word teaching" by wrapping words around sociolinguistic features such as syntax/grammar, morphology, phonetics, semantics, and pragmatics. Ways to select vocabulary; teach before, during, and after reading; and assess vocabulary are part of this chapter.

Chapter 6. Reading in the Content Areas: The deplorable fact that LT-ELs and millions of other students arrive in middle and high school unable to comprehend what they are reading creates a moral obligation for elementary schools to do a better job at teaching reading comprehension, particularly for math, science, and social studies. This chapter highlights key features of reading comprehension and gaps that need to be addressed at K–12 grades for low level readers, as well as instructional strategies and lesson application. It suggests ways to incorporate reading in the content areas for ELs into school improvement plans with five steps for language and literacy development.

Chapter 7. Writing Strategies for ELs and Struggling Writers: This chapter is based on recent meta-analyses of research on writing. It provides learning-to-write and writing-to-learn recommendations on how to adapt the 11 different models of writing for ELs, since the studies of writing have not addressed ELs. Strategies include summarization, collaborative writing, sentence combining, rewriting and inquiry, writing, revising and editing, and the use of rubrics. Our recommendations are based on teacher adaptations and results on the writing outcomes of ELs.

Chapter 8. Engaging ELs via Cooperative Learning and Classroom Management: Cooperative learning has had a strong evidence base for ELs since 1975 (Slavin, 1975) and for ELs since 1990 (Calderón & Carreón, 1994; Calderón & Hertz-Lazarowitz, 1994). It is the best vehicle for ensuring ample EL interaction that leads to more practice of academic language, reading comprehension, and learning of content. This chapter describes how to set up cooperative learning to facilitate classroom management under low anxiety situations and student responsibility for staying on task and learning the assignments in a positive school climate.

Chapter 9. Race to the Top: What Administrators Need to Do: As schools race to become great schools (with or without specific funding), the administrator at the helm needs as much support and tools as do teachers. This chapter and the next two focus on the leadership's role and ways to also become continuous learners and motivators. It offers tips to turn the school improvement plan from an "everything" agenda to a student (LT-ELs) agenda.

Chapter 10. How a Middle School Went From Reconstituted to Highest Performing in Two Years: This chapter, written by an exemplary principal, describes his entry into creating a context of success for his teachers and students and whole school efforts year after year. He offers recommendations for sustainability by creating an ExC-ELL school culture based on his walk-through/instructional rounds, observations, discussions and analyses of teaching and learning.

Chapter 11. Systemic School Reform: Partnering to Ensure EL Success: This chapter, written by a superintendent of a large school district, poses priorities for organizational challenges with a focus on what matters most to close the achievement gap: quality of instruction. He offers recommendations for comprehensive and collaborative systemic changes that are student-centered and meet the district's mission and vision.

Chapter 12. LT-ELs and Core Standards: This concluding chapter captures the essence of this book and addresses the myths that keep the implementation of the core standards to a minimum. It poses "reality" responses with specific recommendations for challenging, rigorous, yet sensitive classroom instruction at the elementary, middle, and high school levels. They are supported by structures and services to accomplish the standards, using the 10 features of school success and fidelity of implementation.

Acknowledgments

We wish to thank the teachers, administrators, and students who contributed to the development and implementation of the ExC-ELL Model.

In Kauai, Hawaii: Kapa'a Middle School and Kapa'a High School and the Kauai District Office;

In New York City: The Office of English Learners, Middle School 319, Middle School 220, and Intermediate School 5;

In Salt Lake City, Utah: Granite Park Middle School, which made adequate yearly progress (AYP) in one year, and

To other schools and districts who are beginning to implement ExC-ELL in Salt Lake City, Milwaukee, McAllen, Brownsville, other New York City schools, and the North Carolina State Department of Education.

We would also like to thank Dan Alpert at Corwin for his tremendous support, care, and expertise in the review and publication of this manuscript.

About the Authors

**Dr. Margarita Calderón** is a professor emerita and senior research scientist at Johns Hopkins University School of Education. She serves on national panels and committees such as the following: National Research Council's Committee on Teacher Preparation, National Literacy Panel for Language Minority Children and Youth, Carnegie Adolescent ELL Literacy Panel, The WIDA Formative Language Assessment Records for ELLs (FLARE) in Secondary School, National Institute for Family Literacy (NIFL) Multicultural Advisory, Professional Advisory Board of the National Center for Learning Disabilities, and ETS Visiting Panel on Research. She is principal investigator in a five-year study in middle and high schools called *ExC-ELL*, on professional development of science, social studies, and language arts teachers of ELs, and *RIGOR*, a curriculum program for teaching language, reading, and content to Students with Interrupted Formal Education (SIFE), ELs in special education, and Newcomers/Refugee ELs, funded by the Carnegie Corporation of New York. She is coprincipal investigator with Robert Slavin on the five-year randomized evaluation of English immersion, transitional, and two-way bilingual elementary programs funded by the Institute for Education Sciences/U.S. Dept. of Education. Other research has been funded by the U.S. Department of Education, U.S. Department of Labor, National Institutes of Health, and Texas Education Agency.

She is the author or coauthor of more than 100 publications. Three recent publications are as follows: *LEAD21 and Science Essentials for ELLs*, a reading series published by McGraw-Hill; *Teaching Reading to English Language Learners, Grades 6–12: A Framework for Improving Achievement in the Content Areas*; and *Designing, and Implementing Two-Way Bilingual Programs*, published by Corwin. She is an international speaker and conducts comprehensive professional development programs throughout the country.

 **Dr. Liliana Minaya-Rowe**, a native of Perú, is currently an educational consultant and a researcher in the areas of teacher education, literacy, two-way bilingual and ESL program design and development, educational leadership, and first and second language acquisition and teaching methodology. She is professor emerita of the Neag School of Education at the University of Connecticut where she implemented a graduate program of specialization in bilingual multicultural education. She taught graduate courses and received and administered 26 U.S. Department of Education grants with multimillion dollar funding from 1980 to 2001. She directed over 42 quasi-experimental and experimental doctoral dissertation research studies in education and graduated 300-plus students at the masters, postmasters, and doctoral levels. She also promoted doctoral graduates' visibility via dissertation research presentations at the American Educational Research Association annual meetings and at state and regional research conferences.

Dr. Minaya-Rowe was coprincipal investigator with Margarita Calderón of the 2003–2008 Johns Hopkins University/Carnegie Corporation of New York *Project ExC-ELL: Expediting Comprehension for English Learners*, to design, implement, and refine a staff development program for middle and high school teachers of literature, science, mathematics, and social studies who have ELs in their classrooms. Dr. Minaya-Rowe edited *Teacher Training and Effective Pedagogy in the Context of Student Diversity*; coauthored with Margarita Calderón, *Raising the Literacy Achievement of English Language Learners* and *Designing and Implementing Two-Way Bilingual Programs*; coauthored with Virginia González and Thomas Yawkey, *English As a Second Language Teaching and Learning: Classroom Applications for Pre-K Through 12th Grade Students*, and she has published over 300 articles, chapters, books, and teacher training manuals and guidebooks.

To my amazing and awesome team: Liliana Minaya-Rowe,
Argelia Carreón,
Elma Noyola, Flo Decker, Maria Trejo, Ana Bishop, Lupita
Espino, Lili Trillo,
Jeanne Cantú, and Luis Mauricio. MC

To my wonderful sisters Yolanda and Beatriz for their love and
support. LMR

1 U.S. Schools Failing ELs

A Call for Change

THE URGENCY FOR CHANGE

An array of reports issued by nationwide committees of education and interdisciplinary experts point to the highest rate of academic failure experienced this decade for upper elementary, middle, and high school English Learners (ELs; Calderón, 2007; Tienda, 2007; U.S. Department of Education, 2007, 2008). Contrary to popular belief, adolescent ELs are not recent newcomers; they have been in U.S. schools since kindergarten! What is wrong with this picture? What has happened or has not happened in our elementary schools that permits this level of failure? Why are secondary school administrators folding their arms and not providing appropriate immediate interventions?

Recent statistical trends in U.S. secondary schools indicate that 80% to 90% of ELs in middle and high school are actually born in the United States. These Long-Term ELs (LT-ELs) are second- or third-generation immigrants. They have attended U. S. schools all their lives, but they have not achieved either high levels of academic English language proficiency or content knowledge to succeed in the all-English mainstream program (Short & Fitzsimmons, 2007).

To complicate matters, the number of ELs in U.S. schools continues to skyrocket. According to the National Clearinghouse for English Language Acquisition (NCELA, 2008), the percentage of mostly Latino ELs in U.S. public schools rose almost 61% between 1995 and 2005, although overall, the total student population growth was 2.6%. There was triple digit growth in 23 states that same time period; 11 of those states saw increases of more than 200%. The Migration Policy Institute (2010) listed other new states such as South Carolina that experienced huge growths in 2007 and 2008. After systematic analysis of demographic trends, Tienda (2007) projects that Latinos will continue to have the highest birthrates until 2030, when they will be the majority in most states and most schools.

The dramatic increase in the EL population caught many states by surprise, particularly those in the Southeast and the Midwest. According to NCELA (2008), Nebraska served a fairly homogeneous White student population until recently. But due in large part to a growing meatpacking industry that employs many Latino workers, the number of ELs grew from approximately 4,000 to more than 16,000 in a 10-year period. ELs now constitute almost 6% of the state's student population. North Carolina has also experienced a dramatic growth of ELs, from approximately 15,000 in 1995 to more than 70,000 in 2005. This growth was due to an increased demand for farm workers, as the state's main agricultural product shifted from tobacco to other crops.

Although states may have been surprised, schools and districts have been overwhelmed by the increases in their EL populations. Not all employ English as a Second Language (ESL) teachers, much less bilingual teachers. In most places, ELs have been placed in mainstream classrooms with teachers who may not be prepared to communicate with and teach ELs. The unexpected and growing numbers of ELs means that these students are no longer only the responsibility of ESL or bilingual teachers. Entire school faculties must serve the ELs, overwhelming mainstream staff.

The Urgency for Older ELs

Older ELs face unique challenges in the nation's schools because of the greater cognitive and linguistic demands of middle and high school. Secondary school ELs must be able to do the following: (a) comprehend, speak, read, and write more advanced course content; and (b) demonstrate deep comprehension on tests that demand advanced English skills. Most ELs have neither the time to catch up to their English-dominant peers, nor been taught the skills necessary to compete academically.

Furthermore, most LT-ELs have not developed high levels of literacy in either their first language or in English. This may be due to the lack of quality and consistent instructional programs that do not allow them to develop academic vocabulary, subject matter concepts, and language proficiency. They need a great deal of help to improve their word knowledge, reading, and writing skills. When the instructional program does not address these needs, students have a very slim chance of closing the achievement gap, promoting to the next grade level, or completing high school requirements. ELs who are new arrivals to this country may not have had sufficient schooling in their countries. Thereby, teachers face added challenges and also need to be prepared to teach this type of student.

If students do not receive high quality instruction and intervention in the elementary grades, early reading problems often develop into serious reading difficulties (Stanovich, 1986). Remediation of reading difficulties for older students is possible in secondary schools, but it is more difficult than preventing the problems through early intervention (Calderón, Hertz-Lazarowitz, & Slavin, 1998; Slavin, 1998; Slavin & Madden, 2001).

This chapter highlights a **theory of action based on empirical evidence** that can be used as a foundation for planning instructional programs and professional development that address the needs of these students. The theory of action is founded on empirical studies of what teachers and educators need to know and on the processes that help transfer knowledge into the teachers' instructional repertoire and thus impact student achievement.

THE ROAD WE'VE TRAVELED ATTEMPTING TO TEACH ELS

We have spent over 40 years attempting to help ELs become bilingual, biliterate, brilliant, and bicultural. In the late 1960s and 1970s, school districts did not have much research on which to build transitional bilingual, dual language, two-way bilingual, or ESL programs. Nevertheless, the need and commitment were there and staff in public schools started taking implementation risks.

In the 1960s and 1970s, elementary schools hired bilingual teachers whose bilingual skills and instructional methods spanned the spectrum from high to low. Additionally, there were too few bilingual teachers to fill the need or vacancies. Teachers were self-taught because universities neither had the preparation programs nor issued bilingual certifications. Teachers had to go to Mexico or Spain or Puerto Rico to buy primary language materials because U.S. publishers did not think it was a good investment to develop and publish them. Yet, educators pushed forward inventing curriculum, instructional strategies, and continua of scope and sequence of language skills development. Thus, programs were developed at the grassroots. Federal funding became available for schools or district personnel who wrote proposals and applied. As long as the funding lasted, so did the programs. Most of the funding went to elementary programs.

Many middle and high schools hired one or two ESL teachers and the curriculum materials were slim pickings. ESL teacher background and methodologies ranged from grammar-based to audio-lingual with many variations of methods in-between. The emphasis was oral language development to help bring ELs up to a conversational level. Since most of the federal funds were devoted to elementary schools, the science of language, literacy, and content as an integral methodology remained untouched. The notion that, in middle and high schools, teachers of math, science, social studies, and language arts needed to embed language and literacy into content was out of the question.

In those early years, professional development approaches were also being invented. State and national associations for second language acquisition and bilingual education were formed and information began to be shared through these grassroots organizations. Other entities such as the Multidistrict Trainer of Trainers Institutes (MTTI), which began in Riverside/San Bernardino, California, and later spread throughout California, began to empirically measure the transfer of training into classroom practices, and new ways of focusing on student outcomes began to emerge (Calderón, 1984, 2008a; Marsh & Calderón, 1989). The MTTI educators also began implementing "coaching of teachers" and "training of literacy coaches" before it became popular. Hence, the notions and practice of comprehensive professional development and coaching were propelled by professionals in the field of ELs far ahead of many others in the early 1980s.

Program evaluation was in its infancy, student assessments to measure growth were nonexistent for ELs, and accountability measures such as those required by No Child Left Behind legislation were nonexistent. However, for the most part, the research community was not focusing on EL issues in those days. A few rigorous controlled studies began to emerge, but most were descriptive in nature. When the time for "proof" came of age in the 2000s, there wasn't much "quantitative" or "scientific" research to back up approaches. Even the most quoted research, regarding which program was more effective for ELs, was a compilation of after-the-fact results devoid of random student assignments, experimental control groups, or pretesting and posttesting. Thus, for many years, the implementation of instructional strategies and program designs were based on what teachers had started 40 years earlier, what was learned at a conference or from a workshop presenter, from the resources available at the schools, and from what schools wanted to adapt (Calderón, 2008a).

CHANGING NOW

After all these decades of "getting by," the schools are confronted with a huge achievement gap between White and Latino students and other minority students. This gap widens as students get older. Adolescent Latino and other minority students have high dropout rates, and there are many high schools with such persistent low rates to be labeled by some as "dropout factories" (Balfanz & Legters, 2004). Drastic reform is being recommended for these high schools. But, as in the 60s and 70s, reform efforts are less than successful. They are not constructed on researched-based practices, and are often layered with political interests instead of educational goals.

The greatest shift in this country's aims derives from the current trend of globalization and the necessity to compete in a "flattened" world within a progressively more integrated world economic system (Friedman, 2005). No longer does the United States remain unchallenged as the greatest economic power. The 21st century has already witnessed a shift in the global marketplace with the United States surrendering its advantage over economic rivals whose levels of educational attainment are surging beyond that of American citizens. Proponents of 21st-century skills assert that "creating an aligned 21st century public education system that prepares students, workers, and citizens to triumph in the global skills race is the central economic competitiveness issue for the next decade" (Partnership for 21st Century Skills, 2008, p. 3) and will require students who can integrate basic skills with content knowledge as well as think independently, solve problems, and make decisions (Johnson, 2009; Rotherham & Willingham, 2009; Silva, 2009).

To meet these needs, policymakers are implementing reform initiatives, and schools are broadening their goals to strengthen academic expectations while encompassing rigorous standards and real-world, problem-solving skills. One indicator of the success of these endeavors is the results of standardized assessments of student performance outcomes.

The United States has participated in international assessments since the 1960s; yet, American students have never fared well in competition (Hanushek, 2004; Koretz, 2009). The most commonly reviewed literacy assessments are the Progress in International Reading Literacy Study (PIRLS) and the Program for International Student Achievement (PISA). Together, these assessments offer a comprehensive understanding of the American education system and its ability to create a competitive workforce for the 21st century.

In analyzing primary school literacy outcomes, PIRLS provides an international comparative study of fourth-grade students' reading literacy. In 2001, the United States placed 12th out of 35 participating education systems, scoring below Lithuania and Hungary (International Association for the Evaluation of Educational Achievement, 2003). PIRLS 2006 results indicate that there was no appreciable change since the previous testing in 2001 (National Center for Education Statistics, 2007, 2009).

PISA assesses academic achievement at the high school level with testing conducted with 15-year olds in reading, math, and science literacy. Sponsored by the Organization for Economic Cooperation and Development (OECD), it was first implemented in 2000. In this context of competing national education systems, the United States placed 15th[h] out of 31 participating countries and last among English-speaking countries in the content area of reading (U. S. Department of Education, 2001). By the 2003 testing cycle, the United States had dropped to 18th out of 41 participating countries (OECD, 2003). In 2006, no reading literacy results were reported due to a printing error in the test booklets (National Center for Education Statistics, 2007). Thus, it's not just ELs whose learning needs must be addressed by our schools. Our attempt with this book is to help schools implement the type of systematic instruction that will help more students succeed—a lot more students!

ADDRESSING THE GAP AND HELPING MORE ELS GRADUATE

Our work with schools also leads us to believe that prevention of LT-ELs and older struggling readers starts at kindergarten. Like all students, ELs need to be able to read something, talk to each other about it, and write about it (Schmoker, 2006). Furthermore, schools need to deliver a content-rich curriculum for all students. Now that more ELs are entering preschool, many believe that we ought to start there.

We cannot continue to do the same things we have been doing. We cannot continue to promote the same programs, curricula, instructional approaches, and evaluation methods. For effective and efficient transformation, we need to become bold and change what needs to be changed from preschool to high school. We need to take a profound look at what we have and then systematically set about changing what needs to change. We need to begin with a theory of change and with the empirical research that supports our theories. Upon these we then develop a plan of action for our schools. Nonetheless, the plan needs to be developed simultaneously by the central district offices, the state department policies and practices, the universities' teacher preparation approaches, the research/evaluation perspectives, and the U. S. Department of Education rules and regulations. We invite everyone to participate in the concerted effort.

A THEORY OF CHANGE BASED ON CURRENT RESEARCH

Three recent seminal reviews of the literature on EL education helped to dispel some long-held myths and brought to light solid research. One review was conducted by the National Literacy Panel on Language Minority Children and Youth (NLP; August & Shanahan, 2006), another by the Center for Research on Education, Diversity, and Excellence (CREDE; Genesse, Lindholm-Leary, Saunders, & Christian, 2006), both published in 2006, and one by the Carnegie Panel on Adolescent EL Literacy, published in 2007 (Short & Fitzsimmons, 2007). The 18 researchers working on the NLP report spent three years identifying studies from 1980 to 2002 that met strict criteria for inclusion in the final report. Studies had to analyze data from experiments or quasi-experiments and include a control or comparison group or random assignments. Out of an original 1,800 publications/studies reviewed, less than 300 met the criteria. From these, CREDE researchers were more inclusive and had their own criteria that enabled them to include more qualitative studies (Genesse et al., 2006). The Carnegie Panel consisted of researchers and practitioners working with adolescent ELs and focused on a few projects and practices that seemed promising (Short & Fitzsimmons, 2007).

Major Findings From the NLP

- Instruction that provides substantial coverage of the key components of reading (phonemic awareness, phonics, fluency, vocabulary, and text comprehension) has clear benefits for language-minority students; however, development of oral proficiency in English is critical along with explicit reading instruction.
- Oral proficiency and literacy in the first language can be used to facilitate literacy development in English.
- Individual differences contribute significantly to English literacy development. Reading difficulties may be more a function of individual differences than of language-minority status.
- Similar proportions of language-minority students and monolingual English speakers are classified as poor readers. Studies revealed that some language-minority students classified as learning disabled can achieve grade-level norms.
- Most assessments do a poor job of gauging individual strengths and weaknesses.
- There is surprisingly little evidence of sociocultural variables on literacy achievement or development. Immigration status, family background, and so forth, do not influence as much as does quality instruction.
- Regardless of the program type (e.g., ESL, transitional bilingual, dual language), what matters most is quality of instruction.

For the complete executive summary, see the Center for Applied Linguistics (http://www.cal.org/projects/archive/nlpreports/Executive_ Summary.pdf). A newer publication entitled, *Developing Reading and*

Writing in Second-Language Learners, extends into implications from the review (see http://www.cal.org).

The CREDE reviews and publications (www.cal.org/crede/pubs/research/rr6.pdf) offer promising practices, but as Goldenberg (2008) admits, the CREDE review did not find any studies that addressed how or even whether progress in the acquisition of English can be accelerated and through what programs. He further asserts that the NLP did not even address this issue (Goldenberg, 2008, p. 12). Thus, the verdict is still out, but we do know what hasn't worked and the basic features that we can use for program development.

The publication, *Double the Work: Challenges and Solutions to Acquiring Language and Academic Literacy for Adolescent English Language Learners—A Report to Carnegie Corporation of New York,* emerged from the Carnegie Panel on Adolescent EL Literacy (Short and Fitzsimmons, 2007; http://www.adlit.org). The 13 panelists provided the following recommendations for practitioners:

- Integrate listening, speaking, reading, and writing skills into instruction from the start.
- Teach the components and processes of reading and writing.
- Teach reading comprehension strategies.
- Focus on vocabulary development.
- Build and activate background knowledge.
- Teach language through content and themes.
- Use native language strategically.
- Pair technology with existing interventions.
- Motivate adolescent ELs through choice.

In this book, we present results and implications for schools from two field studies that integrated these features into models for professional development and curriculum programs. One is *Expediting Comprehension for English Language Learners (ExC-ELL),* developed by Margarita Calderón and colleagues. Over a five-year research study funded by the Carnegie Corporation of New York, ExC-ELL was empirically tested in Kaua'i and New York City schools.

The second research-based curriculum and professional development study, *Reading Instructional Goals for Older Readers* (RIGOR), was created to address the needs of middle and high school ELs/Newcomers/Students with Interrupted Formal Education (SIFE) who are reading at K–3 levels. RIGOR was also developed by Dr. Calderón and published by Benchmark Education Company. It was empirically tested for ELs and struggling readers in 17 middle and high schools in New York City and in three additional schools with special education ELs (SE-ELs).

There are four components of the ExC-ELL and RIGOR staff development programs that also serve as a background of this book: (1) Quality Professional Development, (2) Coaching, (3) Measuring Teacher Implementation and its Impact on Students, and (4) Preparing Administrators to Support and Observe Literacy Instruction in Content Classrooms.

Why Professional Development and Not "An EL Program"?

One important finding from the NLP that needs to be emphasized is the conclusion that regardless of the program being implemented (e.g., ESL, transitional bilingual, dual language), *the most important factor in attaining EL success is quality instruction.* Teacher quality is the one factor everyone agrees has the greatest impact on student learning (Darling-Hammond, 2009; National Reading Panel, 2000; Wright, Horn, & Sanders, 1997). Although there is still questionable data on which program is best for ELs (Genesse et al., 2006; Goldenberg, 2008), we have found that the definitive factor is quality instruction accompanied by quality learning in all classrooms, day by day, minute by minute. *As teachers learn, so do their students.*

Both the NLP and the CREDE reports were concluded in 2003 and 2006, so they did not include in their reviews many of the evidence-based studies that were being conducted at the time or about to be concluded. One set of ongoing longitudinal empirical and randomized studies that were not included (Calderón, 2007, 2008c; Slavin, Madden, Calderón, Chamberlain, & Hennessy, 2010) have identified researched-based instructional strategies that can affect student success in a variety of K–12 school programs.

Through these multiple-year studies, researchers looked at features in elementary, middle, and high schools across the country and found program structures, curriculum components, and professional development designs that work and, of course, some that do not. One prevalent feature of success was that *sustainability of research-based interventions must be accompanied by conscientious accommodations to the particularities, needs, constraints, and resources that occur in a school or district.* It takes extra effort and time on behalf of all school personnel, but they work!

Getting the type of quality teaching and learning you want for your school is highly dependent on the school leader. The school leader becomes fundamental to the changes. The principal of the school will set the culture for continuous professional learning, create the timetable or speed of change, and create expectations for teachers. The principal espouses professional learning that is embedded in the usual practice of the school. There are teams of mainstream, ESL/bilingual, special education teachers working together, planning lessons for ELs, reviewing EL work and progress together, and looking for instructional practices that might be more effective for ELs and all students still struggling.

A Theory of Change

Robust learning and high quality instruction should be the expected outcomes of school practices. ELs should acquire grade level content with high standards in rich learning environments with highly prepared teachers. Continuous progress toward developing academic English, reading comprehension skills, and academic content language are important related goals that should be monitored and assessed until students are achieving. (U.S. Dept. of Education, 2008)

We now have a strong research base upon which to build solid programs for ELs in K–12, unlike in the 1970s and 1980s. We can now provide an understanding and a way to develop a school's theory and infrastructure for addressing EL learning needs. A theory of change helps guide a path and explore goals and ways to attain these. In this book, examples are shared of what has lead exemplary schools (with small or large numbers of ELs) to expedite sustainable change.

A theory of change is a specific and measurable description of a change initiative that forms the basis for strategic planning, for ongoing decision making and evaluation (The Aspen Institute, see http://www .aspeninstitute.org; and the ActKnowledge and Aspen Roundtable, see http://www.theoryofchange.org). A theory of change helps participants do the following:

1. Be clear on long-term goals or desired outcomes.

2. Identify measurable indicators of progress and success/accomplishments/results.

3. Formulate action plans/improvement plans (interventions) to achieve goals.

4. Create a commonly understood vision of all your efforts.

The four procedures apply to schools with small or large groups of ELs. The plan of action will help to address the following:

1. Professional development to set the framework for developing a plan of action

2. Curricula alignment with language proficiency levels, English language proficiency standards, and core content standards—and how all of this comes together

3. The integration of instruction for language, literacy, and content in all classrooms

4. The professional development design for ensuring quality instruction

Addressing Response to Intervention

The theory of change also hinges on the Response to Intervention (RTI) framework and the recent research on struggling readers and on preventing learning disabilities from the National Council on Learning Disabilities (NCLD, 2008). RTI is a three-tier process designed to prevent academic failure or special education labels. It is important to assess how each tier applies to ELs with or without learning disabilities.

RTI acts as a scaffold for teachers to understand their ELs' needs, to develop appropriate methods to address those needs instructionally, and ultimately to determine the difference between an instructional need and an actual disability. Thus, the RTI model enables educators to simultaneously assess ELs' instructional needs and ensure that they receive appropriate daily instruction to promote their literacy skills (Francis, Rivera, Moughamian, & Lesaux, 2008).

Tier 1

All students in Tier 1 receive high quality, scientifically based instruction, differentiated to meet their needs, and are screened on a periodic basis to identify struggling learners who need additional support. Progress of all students is assessed at three points during the school year: fall, winter, and spring. This progress monitoring data should indicate whether ELs and all students are responding adequately to instruction. If not, students are given additional support from a Tier 2 intervention.

Tier 2

In Tier 2, students not making adequate progress in the core curriculum are provided with increasingly intensive instruction matched to their needs on the basis of levels of performance and rates of progress.

Tier 3

At this level, students receive individualized, intensive interventions that target the students' skill deficits for the remediation of existing problems and the prevention of more severe problems. These students participate in daily research-based interventions that are delivered individually or in small groups, and their progress is monitored closely, often once or twice a week.

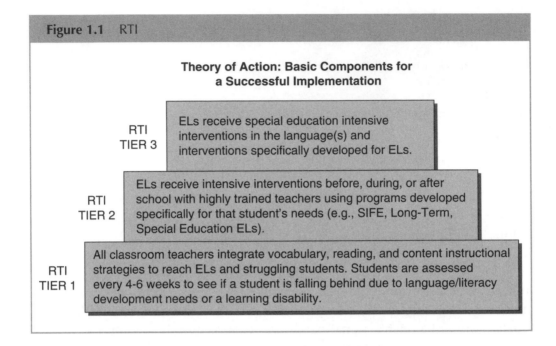

Figure 1.1 RTI

Theory of Action: Basic Components for
a Successful Implementation

RTI
TIER 3

ELs receive special education intensive interventions in the language(s) and interventions specifically developed for ELs.

RTI
TIER 2

ELs receive intensive interventions before, during, or after school with highly trained teachers using programs developed specifically for that student's needs (e.g., SIFE, Long-Term, Special Education ELs).

RTI
TIER 1

All classroom teachers integrate vocabulary, reading, and content instructional strategies to reach ELs and struggling students. Students are assessed every 4-6 weeks to see if a student is falling behind due to language/literacy development needs or a learning disability.

THE THEORY OF CHANGE ASSUMPTIONS

Our theory of change is based on the following key assumptions. ELs can be successful, if the program that a school establishes provides a variety of interventions focusing on individual needs, because not all ELs need the same intervention.

> Teachers and specialists who are highly prepared to impart evidenced-based instructional practices conduct these programs.
> Only evidence-based instructional programs proven to work with similar ELs in those grade levels is implemented by schools.
> Teachers only use researched-based instructional strategies in their repertoire.
> The teachers are well supported by their administration and work collaboratively to improve learning for all students.
> The focus for everyone in the school is not necessarily on "teaching" but on student "learning" and "outcomes."
> Quality teaching is not an end in itself; it is a vehicle to attain terrific student learning outcomes.

Setting High Expectations With Equally High Support

Interaction and collegial skills appear to be a positive trademark of great school leaders. Boyatzis and McKee (2005) describe resonant leadership as those leaders who bring out the best in people and inspire those around them. They help to dispel fears and despair and replace those with hope, compassion, and risk-taking.

ELs can be successful if

1. Appropriate programs are offered to address the diverse backgrounds of ELs.

2. EL programs are comprehensible and schoolwide.

3. EL instruction is based on evidence that it works for them.

4. Principals convey the importance of rigorous quality teaching and continuous professional learning.

5. All their teachers know how to provide effective instruction and are sensitive to their cultural and background knowledge.

6. Vital participation from school, district, and state administrators is in place.

7. They know you care for them.

8. You are not afraid to take that first step.

Questions and Topics for Discussion

1. What works for ELs?
2. What are the changes you need to make to adjust that paradigm?
3. What are the implications from this chapter for your school?
4. What would take these ideas to another level?

2 The ELs

THE DIVERSITY OF ELS

ELs are not a homogeneous group. The students differ in various ways, including level of oral English proficiency, literacy and academic ability in both their native language and English, and cultural backgrounds. English learners born in the United States often develop conversational language abilities in English but lack academic language proficiency. Newcomers, on the other hand, might need to develop both conversational and academic English.

Education previous to entering U.S. schools helps determine students' literacy levels in their native language. Some learners have limited or no literacy because of the quality of previous schooling, interrupted schooling due to wars or migration, and other circumstances. Given the wide range of English learners and their backgrounds, it is important that all teachers take the time to learn about their students, particularly in terms of their literacy histories.

A Spectrum of ELs

1. ELs in preschool and K–3

2. Newcomers—Well-Schooled

3. Migrant students

4. LT- ELs

5. Reclassified ELs or upper elementary, middle, and high school ELs who are attending mainstream classrooms and not receiving special services

6. Struggling readers who are not ELs for various reasons

7. Newcomers—SIFE or Refugees

8. SE-ELs

One similarity these groups share is the need to explicitly develop academic English, reading comprehension skills, and content knowledge in order to achieve academically and to graduate from high school.

Profiles of ELs

A. ELs in Preschool–Third Grade

The number of words heard in an hour by children of poverty is about 615, by middle class children about 1,251, and by children of professionals about 2,153 (Hart & Risley, 1995). The average 6-year-old has a vocabulary of approximately 8,000 words (Senechal & Cornell, 1993). However, if the students' primary language is not English, the student comes to school needing extensive vocabulary in order to add those 8,000 words in English. It is critically important to do so in the early years because vocabulary in kindergarten and first grade is a significant predictor of reading comprehension in the middle and secondary grades (Cunningham, 2005; Cunningham & Stanovich, 1997) or reading difficulties (Chall & Dale, 1995).

B. Newcomers—Well-Schooled

While the LT-ELs are the large majority of ELs in U.S. schools, the remaining ELs are Newcomers. Newcomers are refugees, immigrants, or recent arrivals. Some Newcomers have high literacy skills in their native language and can benefit from accelerated language proficiency skills. These well-educated Newcomers sometimes know more about math, science, world history, and geography than their English-speaking peers. They expect to be challenged through a rigorous curriculum.

C. Migrant, Transient, and Transnational Students

These students have been migrating from state to state and within states with their parents, following harvesting schedules and work opportunities. In many cases, these are the brilliant students who have so much worldly knowledge that they learn quickly and become the recipients of scholarships to top universities. Their parents have a focused goal of helping them succeed, no matter the cost. In other cases, the struggles for day-to-day living are too overwhelming and students may not have the privilege of systematic school attendance. Thus, migrant students can be SIFE, LT-ELs, or class valedictorians.

Unfortunately, many families also migrate from one part of the city to another in search of better housing opportunities or jobs. They move around in the same district or neighboring school districts. They return to the same schools several times.

Other families spend several months or years in their country of origin before they return to the U.S. schools. Maneuvering between two different school systems and languages can take a toll on students and their parents.

D. LT-ELs

LT-ELs are students who are in school systems for seven or more years without passing tests that would get them out of the category. These are ELs who have been in and out of various instructional programs (e.g., sheltered English, ESL/content-based ESL, ESL pull out/push in, transitional bilingual education, structured English immersion, bilingual special education, etc.) without having benefited from any kind of continuous and sustained instructional support program. They were born and raised in the United States and have attended U.S. schools since kindergarten. Some might have had low attendance. They are usually below grade level in reading, writing, and math, and do poorly on standardized tests. Their primary language is usually limited to social conversations, lacking in academic discourse, grammar, reading, and writing skills.

Most LT-ELs have the English conversational and social fluency in English but lack the grade-level academic language proficiency (vocabulary, high literacy levels, grammar, and writing) that is necessary to compete with native English speakers and to succeed in mainstream English classrooms. They are typically socially, psychologically, and educationally isolated from mainstream students and in urgent need of effective approaches, strategies, and curriculum that will help them catch up to and compete with mainstream students. Their motivation may have been hampered, but they can be brought back as soon as they believe that they can be successful students.

E. Reclassified ELs

Reclassified ELs are those who are no longer receiving services because they have been reclassified based on a test of language proficiency. These students are in mainstream classrooms in upper elementary, middle, or high schools. However, they usually continue to struggle in reading, writing, and math, and they score low on standardized tests. They may begin at grade level but soon start falling behind as the content gets more difficult. Their teachers may be passing them with average grades because they behave well, do the required assignments and schoolwork. Their grades often give students and their parents/guardians the false impression of their academic achievement.

Reclassified ELs may have English conversational skills and social fluency in English, but they lack the grade-level academic language proficiency (e.g., vocabulary, high literacy levels, grammar, writing) necessary to compete with native English speakers and to succeed in mainstream English classrooms.

F. Struggling Readers Not Classified As ELs

Struggling readers may or may not be ELs. Some language-minority students were never identified by schools through official processes. They fell through the cracks when it came to assessments. Others are English-speaking, native-born, struggling readers. For example, in some Hawaiian schools, about 85% of the students speak Hawaiian Creole. Alaska has students who have Native American language backgrounds, and inner cities have African American students who may need to strengthen their academic English. All struggling readers, just as ELs, are in need of effective academic, social, and cognitive skills, as well as rigorous instruction to enable them to succeed in school. Their low reading level limits their thinking, problem solving, and other cognitive abilities that are grade-level appropriate.

G. Newcomers—Students with Interrupted Formal Education (SIFE) or Refugees

Some Newcomers at the 3rd- through 12th-grade levels are also called Students with Interrupted Formal Education (SIFE). The New York State Department of Education explains SIFE this way:

> SIFE students usually bring limited or interrupted formal schooling in their home countries. They have low levels of literacy and content background knowledge in their home language. Their needs surpass the resources of regular ESL or bilingual programs. The older SIFE will need intensive interventions to catch up with basic skills.

The background knowledge Newcomers such as SIFE or Refugee children bring to school greatly affects their performance. For this reason, teachers of English learners should be sure to build background for content lessons rather than assuming that Newcomers come with the same background knowledge as mainstream students or that of ELs who have lived in this country all their lives.

H. SE-ELs

Some ELs may bring exceptional education needs, as their mainstream counterparts. Recognized disabilities include the following, among others:

specific learning disabilities, speech or language impairment, mental retardation, hearing impairment, serious emotional disturbance, multiple disabilities, visual impairment, deaf/blindness, and autism.

There continues to be an overrepresentation of ELs in special education programs, and there are still cases in which ELs are placed in special education programs due to their lack of English proficiency. ELs experiencing academic difficulties are sometimes placed in special education programs without any specialized services. There are some disabilities that are difficult to define and identify. Unlike physical conditions that are more objectively verifiable, many learning disabilities are still assessed through observation, judgment, or ambiguous tests. The inability to distinguish between a learning disability and language proficiency is a key problem. Consequently, some ELs are diverted from opportunities while others fail to get the help they need.

Response to Intervention (RTI), discussed in Chapter 1, is a different way of looking at learning problems. Instead of first identifying students as having a learning disability, this process recommends various supports and quality instruction to address potential deficiencies. Only if the student fails to respond to repeated interventions does the school team consider special placement.

SO MANY LT-ELS

They represent the largest EL subgroup in most schools and school districts. Their elementary education did not serve them well. When we interviewed many of these students, we found out that their education had been stifled due to several reasons. These are some of the reasons shared:

1. Inconsistencies with language policy and attention to ELs, such as the following

   o ELs attended kindergarten in English (L2), then first and second grade in Spanish (L1), followed by third grade in English.
   o ELs were immersed in English from K–5 with no support in Spanish or ESL.
   o ELs were in all-Spanish instruction in K–4 with only 30 minutes a day in English, then they were immersed in English in the fifth grade.
   o ELs were in all-Spanish instruction in K–5 with 60 minutes for ESL, but they were not taught to read in English; the teachers read to them. When they went to middle school, they could not read the textbooks.
   o Were promoted from year to year even with such low grades as Ds and Fs

2. Low quality instruction as described by the LT-ELs:

○ "When I reached seventh grade, I couldn't understand what I was reading, so they put me in the same phonics program I had in K–3."

○ "We never read science or social studies books in my elementary school—only little stories."

○ "The teacher left me alone because he would sit in the back of the room, quietly, and I never looked at the teacher."

○ "Another teacher would come into my classroom to translate what the teacher was saying, so I didn't have to learn English."

We discovered other reasons as we visited schools and interviewed teachers. Some of these are cited here:

- "K–3 reading program in English with materials that were not developed for ELLs; could read very fast but couldn't understand what she was reading."
- "Most of our teachers were not ESL credentialed; they had never even taken a course on second language instruction. There was no one to help the students besides me."
- "Our principals came and went, and we changed programs and curriculum every year; no stability whatsoever."
- "I got tired of teaching in trailers. We were always segregated. My self-esteem was suffering as much as the children's."
- "We had a great bilingual program; then it was dismantled. This created an emotional and instructional gap for years."
- "Many of our students were not identified as ELs so they were placed in mainstream classrooms—sink or swim!"
- "I had the whole gamut of ELs in my classroom; some were Long Term, but I had to teach to the middle."
- "The older students are really nice but they don't participate in class. I can't seem to get them engaged in reading."
- "They want to go to college but they have such huge gaps."

REPAIRING OR AVOIDING DAMAGE TO ELS

How do we repair or avoid damage to ELs? First, we need to learn all we can about each individual child and family. We need to know what is the best instructional placement for their needs. The assessments currently used for placement need to go beyond oral English or number of words a student can read per minute. We need to know the depth and breadth of their academic language that consists of morphology, syntax, phonetics, semantics, and pragmatics:

> Morphology—study of the forms of words (root words, affixes)
> Syntax—the arrangement of words and phrases to create well-formed sentences
> Phonetics—the study and classification of speech sounds
> Semantics—logical aspects of meaning, such as sense, reference, implication, word relations (collocation), and the cognitive structure of meaning
> Pragmatics—context for language use, including discourse or text organization, turn-taking in conversations, presupposition, and implicature

Therefore, we need to assess (a) their vocabulary bank in English and in their primary language that includes different types of words, receptive and productive use of phrases, idioms, cognates, multiple meaning words, and so forth; (b) their reading comprehension level in English and in their primary language; (c) their knowledge and application of grammar and writing; and (d) their knowledge of math, science, and social studies and the language to express cognitive and academic functions. (These features of language and literacy are further explained in Chapters 6–8). If we only test oral language, we do not get a full picture.

Once we have a better assessment process and better identification of our students' characteristics, we can proceed to develop a plan for their instruction through questions such as the following:

• What are the student configurations of the classrooms per grade level?
• What type of program(s) do we need to address the diversity of student needs?
• What are the expectations of my school? Do I want students to be fully bilingual? Do we only use their primary language as support? Is it impossible to provide primary language support because there are so many languages?
• How many teachers do we need to hire?
• What specific professional development programs do we offer?
• What curriculum, textbook levels, and ancillary materials do we need to purchase?

Forms such as Figure 2.1 and Figure 2.2 can be used to build a profile of a student or a group of ELs. The profiles can give quick glimpses of the

Figure 2.1 The Diversity of ELs in K–5

Type of Intensive Intervention Necessary	Grades PreK–3	Grades 4–5 Newcomer (2 or less years in the U.S.), SIFE	Grades 4–5 Newcomer (2 or less years in the U.S.), Well-Schooled	Grades K–5 Migrant, Reclassified ELs, Struggling Readers	Grades K–5 SE-ELs
Culture of schooling; learning styles and study skills	20	4	4	8	2
Phonemic awareness	15	4	2	5	2
Phonics, decoding, fluency	20	4	2	5	2
Primary language vocabulary tiers 1, 2, 3 (see Chapter 5)	9	3	0	3	2

numbers and types of students to be placed in different classes. Additionally, it helps a school identify the specific interventions for SIFE, highly schooled Newcomers, LT-ELs, SE-ELs, or ELs in mainstream classes. No one single class fits all student profiles. In addition to recording the number of student characteristics for each grade level, the chart can also be used to plot the complete profile of a classroom. Figure 2.1 contains an example of how many students need what types of specific intensive interventions. For example, in PreK–3, 20 children would need to know about the culture of schooling, since they are new to the school system. By the same token, four SIFE or four well-schooled Newcomers would also need to know the protocols and learning styles of the school. Additionally, eight migrant students and two special education students would also need help establishing those habits of schooling. This will help them develop learning strategies early on in preparation for high school and college. The next intervention is "phonemic awareness." which may be important for beginning students but not so much for well-schooled or reclassified ELs. Thus, regardless of the numbers of identified ELs in each student category, not all those will need the same type of intervention. Figure 2.2 gives a similar example for ELs in ninth grade.

Figure 2.2 An Example of a Profile of Ninth Graders

Type of Intensive Intervention Necessary	Newcomers (2 or less years in the U.S.)		LT-ELs (20 students)	SE-ELs (4 students)
	SIFE (10 students)	Well-Schooled (5 students)		
Culture of schooling	3			2
Phonemic awareness	5	5	4	3
Phonics	5	2	12	4
Primary language vocabulary tiers 1, 2, 3	8			4
English vocabulary tiers 1, 2, 3	10	5	(tiers 2 & 3) 20	4
Grammar	10	5	15	4
Discourse	10	5	5	3
Reading comprehension strategies	7	3	20	4
Basic writing mechanics	7	2	20	4
Literature	10	5	15	4
Math	9	1	17	4
Science	10	2	20	4
Social Studies	10	5	20	4
Study skills	5		20	4

Indicate with a 🗐 what additional assessment or intervention is needed.

"If we want not merely to improve but to maximize the college and career readiness of U.S. students, we need to intervene not only during high school but also before high school in the upper elementary grades and in middle school" (ACT, 2008).

YOUR TURN!

In your study group, determine the diversity of your EL population and the configurations for your instructional targets using the chart in Figure 2.3 or a similar one.

Figure 2.3 Range of ELs and Type of Intervention Each Student Might Need

Type of Necessary Intensive Intervention	Grades PreK–3	Newcomers (2 or less years in the U.S.) Grades 4–12		LT-ELs, Migrant, Reclassified ELs, Struggling Readers	SE-ELs
		SIFE	Well-Schooled		
Culture of schooling					
Phonemic awareness					
Phonics, decoding, fluency					
Primary language vocabulary tiers 1, 2, 3					
English vocabulary tiers 1, 2, 3					

Questions and Topics for Discussion

1. Outline the profiles for the ELs at your school with a focus on their literacy histories.
2. What are the changes in the school improvement plan to address the interventions and instructional targets needed to give ELs access to the best education you can offer?
3. How would this chapter inform your school's theory of action and change?

3 Tools for Schools

The Framework for
Preventing LT-ELs

TEN KEY FACTORS LEADING TO STUDENT SUCCESS

A comprehensive, professional development effort, the fourth key feature of student success, is a requirement for effective implementation of any new instructional program. This chapter is devoted to a discussion of an evidence-based professional development program that is comprehensive in its content and process and includes training educators in the use of an observational protocol to measure transfer from training and impact on students.

In a recent study, the students in both Sheltered English Instruction (SEI) and Transitional Bilingual Education (TBE) programs did equally well because the schools adhered to the concept of *10 components or factors of quality instruction, professional development, and school structures* (Calderón & Slavin, 2010; Slavin et al., in press). Each one is briefly described here, with some examples. While these features are specific to elementary schools, similar ones have been identified in another longitudinal study in middle and high schools (Calderón, 2007).

This study compared the English and Spanish language and reading performance of Spanish-dominant children randomly assigned beginning in kindergarten, to TBE or Dual Language (DL) or SEI in six schools in six states. All schools had similar student populations of Latino students, with an average of 58% ELs. This is the first randomized study to compare TBE and SEI reading approaches over a period as long as five years. On the Peabody Picture Vocabulary Test (PPVT) and its Spanish equivalent (TVIP) and on English and Spanish versions of three Woodcock Reading Scales, kindergartners and first graders in TBE/DL performed significantly better in Spanish and worse in English than their SEI counterparts, as expected. After transitioning to English, TBE children in Grades 2 to 4 scored significantly lower than those in SEI on the measure of receptive vocabulary, the PPVT, but there were no significant differences on most English reading measures. On the Spanish language (TVIP) and reading measures, TBE students scored significantly higher than SEI in Grades K–3 but not Grade 4. Both groups gained substantially in English receptive language skills over the years. These findings suggest that Spanish-dominant students learn to read in English equally well in TBE/DL and SEI. When quality instruction is offered, students transfer skills between each language, and both languages are enhanced.

The findings of the study reinforced the frequently stated conclusion that what matters most in the education of ELs is the quality of instruction (August & Shanahan, 2006, 2008), not the language of instruction. Schools may choose to teach ELs in either their native language or in English for many reasons, including cultural, economic, or political rationales.

Bilingual programs bring benefits to students, schools, and families such as cognitive advantages, academic success, family ties, career advantages, personal well-being, and of course, bilingualism (Cummins, 1981). Children can attain all these benefits only if they continue to have their Spanish developed through academic language and domain specific knowledge, especially as they move up through the grades (August, Goldenberg, & Rueda, 2010; August & Shanahan, 2006). When there are multiple language groups in a school or not enough bilingual teachers for a bilingual program, schools can implement a quality SEI program. However, there was no support in the study for the idea that low quality "sink or swim" immersion works. The SEI programs adhered to the same 10 key features, as did the TBE or DL programs; in particular, all teachers in a school received extensive training and follow-up coaching, plus monitoring for fidelity and quality. Adjustments for fidelity and quality of teaching were continuously made, while students were assessed to address the correlation between teaching and learning.

TEN FEATURES OF SCHOOL SUCCESS AND EFFECTIVE IMPLEMENTATION

1. School structures

The school structures are the cornerstones for school improvement. The structures include orchestrating, monitoring, and constantly upgrading all the features mentioned from numbers 2 to 10. They include instituting Teacher Learning Communities by grade levels or subject areas where teachers can share, solve problems, and create meaningful lessons. There should be study groups that delve into research and best practices to make recommendations on improvements in the 10 features/components of school improvement.

2. Language, literacy, and subject domain instructional components

These are described in further detail in Chapters 4 through 8. They sustain the premise that language, literacy, and content learning are an integrated approach to learning for ELs and for all students. Teachers who adopted this approach found that all students benefit and enhance their learning.

3. Equitable materials in L1 and L2

School and classroom libraries and textbooks exist that represent different cultures and facilitate learning in English and Spanish. Unfortunately, publishers still shy away from other languages, but as the demand grows, so do the volumes. Equitable materials also means providing quality materials for SIFE, special education, and Newcomer students who need specialized texts at their levels and that can quickly take them to higher levels. An ESL textbook for intermediate ELs will not meet their needs.

4. Comprehensive professional development

A comprehensive professional development encompasses intensive training institutes at the beginning of the year, follow-up coaching for all teachers, refresher workshops, and observation protocols to measure instructional efficacy, fidelity of implementation, and ongoing influences on student performance. This chapter goes into further detail later.

5. Leadership

Leaders "move" individuals, institutions, and whole systems forward. They know a great deal about positive motion and how to deal with the frustrations of lack of movement (Fullan, 2010, p. 2). When learning and doing is the purpose of the school, there isn't one right way of generating positive motion. We add aspects of leadership throughout this book that we have gathered through our work with hundreds of schools in (as we hate to admit) the last 40 years. The last two chapters encapsulate the perspective of two great change leaders—a principal and a superintendent.

6. Parent/family support teams

Engaging parents in schools is not easy. Engaging language-minority parents in schools may appear even harder, but these are parents that value their children's education just as much or even more than mainstream parents. Schools can attract parents when they provide training for teachers on how to work with parents and for parents on how to become meaningfully involved with the school and the education of their children. Family support committees can also be established to attend to issues of student underachievement, low attendance, tardiness, health, and other family issues.

7. Tutoring

Some students will need additional assistance with vocabulary or reading or writing. We must not let them fall through the cracks on their way to learning. Intensive immediate interventions need to be designed and ready to roll when a student needs help. Schedules such as before or after school, Saturday academies, and summer school sessions need to be in place with qualified staff.

8. Benchmark assessments

Benchmark and performance assessments have become the norm. It is no longer smart to wait for end-of-the-year test results to gauge student learning. The new systems of evaluation need to work for, rather than against, students. The assessments should support teaching rather than distract from it. They should reflect the core standards, help raise achievement, and increase equity. The systems of evaluation should include (a) distributed accountability exams, given periodically during the school year that should be educative for both students and teachers; (b) a formative assessment for teachers to use to develop learning profiles of each student; and (c) a technology platform that makes it easy for schools and teachers to have immediate feedback on what is working or needs fixing (Resnick & Berger, 2010). For years, programs such as Success for All have had benchmark assessments and observational tools that helped schools determine which students needed tutoring, when to discontinue tutoring, and when to move a student to a higher level. Observation checklists also gave the schools a profile of the instructional efficacy in each classroom. As new assessment systems are being developed for the core standards and policies, it is very likely that these research-based features will be part of those policies and practices. The continuation of this chapter outlines a system that has been tested in middle and high schools with EL populations.

9. Coaching of teachers

Coaching helps change the culture of teaching and learning. It creates fidelity with ownership and fidelity to an innovation. It helps sustain quality implementation. When done right, coaching helps everyone become a learner—the observed and the observer. It is a vehicle for updating the curriculum. Most important, it improves student achievement. However, coaching can become a superficial endeavor. Many recent studies have found no effects from coaching. Therefore, it is important to treat it as a teaching/learning intervention and—do it right.

10. Monitoring implementation

Although coaching helps teachers develop quality teaching, it is also important to monitor the implementation of the innovation and the 10 features of quality schooling. Later we describe a process for monitoring effective teaching and the ongoing classroom performance of students. Through technology, we are able to capture, analyze, and create different types of data summaries for teachers, coaches, and administrators. Monitoring will be a major piece of any new legislation. Accountability will need back-up data on all school components, particularly how daily instruction affects learning for all students.

The Relationship Between Characteristics of Professional Development and Student Learning

What are some ways that professional development leads to measureable improvements in student learning? There are many issues that impact the connection between student learning and teacher preparation (National Research Council, 2010). Designing effective professional development by schools and school districts is often a complex undertaking. Schools need to begin by establishing clear causal links between their particular teachers' needs, their teacher preparation offerings, and their student outcomes. Schools differ in the types of teachers they attract—the types of knowledge and skills that teachers bring and what they acquire in the school. Due to the variability, using only measures of student outcomes on standardized achievement scores will not give a clear picture of teacher effectiveness and their connection to student learning.

A better connection between student learning and teacher effectiveness can be made by observing teacher knowledge and skills and the delivery of those skills in the classroom. The use of observational protocols that measure various domains of teaching have been linked to student outcomes in several recent studies (Calderón, 2007; Grossman et al., 2009; Pianta & Hamre, 2009). Observational protocols offer a vehicle for exploring the contributions of teacher preparation and evaluating teachers' effectiveness (National Research Council, 2010).

An observation protocol that has been tested for validity and reliability in the diverse EL population classrooms from Hawaii to Salt Lake City to New York is the ExC-ELL Observation Protocol (EOP). The pilot and replication of its use has given teachers and students an effective picture of teacher and student interaction around teaching/learning events for vocabulary, discourse, reading comprehension, writing, cooperative learning, classroom management, and content learning. It provides guidance on what is effective and what needs improvement. In other words, it answers the teacher question, "Is my teaching reaching?"

The EOP helps everyone get on board for that journey into continuous improvement. It sets a common ground for all teachers and administrators to share the same language and approach to performance assessment for positive change. The integration of language, literacy, and content means that, although the ESL/bilingual staff may have been the language experts and in charge of EL instruction for the most part, they may need to know more about teaching reading comprehension or content academic vocabulary/language. Mainstream teachers may know which key vocabulary is important to teach in each subject area, but they may not know the syntactical structures or problematic words that nest those key content words and create difficulties for ELs. Reading specialists and special education teachers who have been in charge of RTI Tier 2 and 3 interventions may also need to know current strategies to accelerate learning for ELs and other students. In other words, all teachers may need to know new developments in EL pedagogy, technology, and performance assessment. Literacy coaches and school administrators need to know how to observe and give feedback to all teachers who have the diversity of ELs.

Purposes of the ExC-ELL Protocol (EOP)

- To use as a teacher guide for planning lessons
- For teachers to reflect on their own instruction after a lesson
- To do authentic assessment/performance assessment and keep track of student progress
- For peer coaching—visiting each other's classrooms and helping to implement ExC-ELL or any other instructional approach with fidelity and creativity

- To use as a tool for professional conversations in Teacher Learning Communities
- For coaches to observe teachers and students and give on-target feedback
- For principals, assistant principals, and administrators to observe teachers and students and give on-target feedback
- To conduct classroom action research, particularly for those teachers seeking a higher degree
- To use as a performance assessment tool for keeping track of the correlation between quality instruction and impact on students through different types of EOP reports—by grade level, by language/literacy/content components, by teacher, by quarters, semester, or end-of-the-year reports. The systematic data on classroom implementation provide a real-time photograph of any classroom or a photo composition of each classroom for the year

The EOP can be used either as a paper or an electronic instrument. In the electronic version, a digital pen is used to record and transfer data (on student and/or teacher performance) onto a computer for charting progress and outcomes online. Some schools prefer to keep the data anonymous; others use students' names to track specific continuous growth. Either way, the data graphs help teachers, coaches, and administrators have a clear focus on the learning goals and the progress made on a continuous basis for each goal.

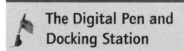

The Digital Pen and Docking Station

Training of Teachers, Coaches, and Peer Coaches

It is important to provide preparation and practice to use such performance tools. Through the ExC-ELL Institutes, teachers learn all the components of the EOP and how to deliver those components through instructional options. First, teachers learn the theory, the research, and the why, what, and how of the integrated instruction at the Institute. They also have the opportunity to bring their textbooks and practice using the EOP as a lesson template for planning their lessons and then reflecting after each lesson on the delivery of its components. The template also gives both coach and teacher an observable objective measure on which to make connections between teaching and learning. In addition, it helps teachers focus on specific, reachable goals to practice for the next observation.

With the EOP, coaches learn how to observe instruction on vocabulary, oracy, reading, writing, cooperative learning, and classroom management.

Coaches learn how to give technical feedback that is nonthreatening through a cycle of preconferences, observational data collection, feedback, teacher reflection, and goal setting. Coaches learn how to inspire teachers to reflect on their teaching and to take action that leads students closer to their learning goals.

Student Performance and Online Assessment Tools

The observation protocol also becomes a value-added assessment that measures individual student performance year after year to compare with other assessments or standardized assessments. Coupled with common school assessments, these performance measures help teachers gauge student understanding by identifying ways to help the students and giving feedback to the students so they can focus on those skills that need to be fine-tuned before a test or move to the next level. Teachers learn how to use the EOP, along with observational skills, to give feedback and help students set goals for achievement. ESL, bilingual, and sheltered instruction teachers, as well as math, science, social studies, and language arts teachers, have used the pen to study their craft.

School Leadership

Administrators and specialists have reported this training as valuable because it focuses not only on content instruction but also on literacy, language, and content development, and it actually applies to all students, not just ELs. The training also provides field experiences for principals as they shadow the trainers and practice observing, collecting data, interpreting, and giving feedback to teachers.

Principals, assistant principals, and teacher leaders learn how effective, empirically tested instruction for ELs also helps the rest of the student population attain higher levels of academic achievement. School leaders learn how the EOP, as a formative assessment tool, has the ability to transform the way teachers teach and students learn. The leadership team learns the following:

- How to gauge when students are and are not learning and how to promote adjustments to instruction or EL program structures
- How to establish a collaborative climate in the school through effective Teacher Learning Communities
- How to support and sustain continuous teacher professional development

OVERVIEW OF THE EVIDENCE-BASED PROFESSIONAL DEVELOPMENT COMPONENTS

Before using the observation protocol, all teachers, coaches, and administrators attend a comprehensive professional development Institute and follow-up activities on evidence-based pedagogy focusing on ELs and struggling readers. The pedagogy and professional development framework is based on the longitudinal study of the professional development model, *Expediting Comprehension for English Language Learners* (ExC-ELL; Calderón, 2007; Calderón, Minaya-Rowe, Carreón, Durán, & Fitch, 2009a, b). This quantitative and qualitative study provided great insights into change efforts and professional growth struggles. Math, science, social studies, and language arts teachers who had ELs in their classrooms gladly, painfully, and reluctantly tried different approaches for selecting and teaching vocabulary/language functions, reading comprehension strategies and skills, and writing techniques for their different subject areas. After testing different combinations for years, they helped us find ways of enhancing oral language and use of academic language that built upon the students' literacy and content learning.

Great results were attained only by those schools that adhered fidelity to the model, all components, and time recommended for teachers to integrate all into their teaching repertoires and lesson plans. Teachers were also given weekly time to meet in their Teacher Learning Communities to further their understanding and skill and thus sustain the quality of implementation.

As a follow-up to this project, funded by the Carnegie Corporation of New York (Calderón, in press; Calderón et al., 2009a), we began scaling up ExC-ELL and have since offered the professional development program and on-site follow-up activities in various schools, school districts, regional educational centers, and universities for teams of teachers, coaches, and administrators. The professional development components are described here to help schools analyze their own professional development, to build upon what is already working or to start from scratch and create more meaningful professional development plans (Calderón, 2007; Calderón, in press; Calderón et al., 2009a). At the end of the chapter, there is a chart that you can use to draw comparisons between the current professional development that is offered by your school or school district and the practices that research has proven effective.

Professional Development Participants Who Attend the Same Sessions

> Mainstream teachers who have or will have one or more ELs and struggling readers; ESL, dual language, special education, and reading specialists; and literacy coaches
> Administrators from schools with low and high EL populations

Target Students

Target students include the following: LT-ELs, highly schooled Newcomers, SIFE, Refugees, SE-ELs, migrant students, struggling readers or students reading below grade level, gifted and talented students, and mainstream students.

Desired Outcomes for the Professional Development

Through the various instructional tasks and activities, students are introduced to, and practice, a full range of reading skills and different types and levels of vocabulary/language complexity. They build fluency, read extensively, and master the concepts/content they are reading across the content areas. The writing is connected to the subject-area required writing style and technique.

Initial Institutes. At least 40 hours of initial professional development is required to facilitate the teachers' development of the skills, confidence, and efficacy in teaching the knowledge and skills required for the desired outcome. For example, the professional development for ExC-ELL is a comprehensive program consisting of an initial five-day institute where trainers do the following:

- Present theory and research for each instructional component (vocabulary/grammar, oracy, reading, writing, cooperative learning, classroom management)
- Model strategies for each component
- Give participants time to debrief, ask questions, and practice with peers
- Provide time to integrate new strategies into their lessons/content areas
- Ask schools to give teachers an additional three to five days to work in their learning communities to develop additional lessons

On-Site Follow-Up. After the five-day institute, the follow-up consists of three or more visits to each teacher's classroom during the year and follow-up, refresher, miniworkshops by ExC-ELL expert coaches. School coaches are encouraged to shadow the ExC-ELL coaches and participate in Coaching Institutes of one additional day after the five-day institute. Administrators and other school leaders are encouraged to attend the five-day institute and one additional day of training on *Building Teacher Support Systems in the School.* At the five-day institute and the follow-up school visits, the school leader, coaches, and teachers also learn how to structure and work effectively in learning communities. They learn to use performance assessment tools and records of progress to keep track of their students' progress toward their goals.

Expected Outcomes from the Professional Development for Teachers and Students

The design of the professional development uses the sequence of the teachers' lessons: vocabulary, reading, writing, anchoring of content knowledge, and assessment. The objectives or outcomes for these instructional domains are delivered in five phases.

Phase 1

Students. In Phase 1, students learn vocabulary words from different categories that have been selected by their teachers from the texts they are about to read.

Teachers. In this phase, teachers learn to select words to teach according to their students' language and reading levels. The words range from easy to sophisticated to content-specific, concept-laden words and words that nest those concepts. Teachers learn how to orchestrate vocabulary practice and mastery, discourse protocols, and word analysis activities before, during, and after reading. Teachers also practice syntactic processing so that they can teach the ways that grammar knowledge supports reading comprehension.

Coaches and Administrators. Coaches and administrators learn how to observe vocabulary instructional delivery and how students apply new words. They learn how to give effective feedback on depth and breadth of word usage.

Phase 2

Students. In Phase 2, students are introduced to and apply reading strategies that support comprehension and subject domain mastery.

Teachers. Teachers learn how to model through "think-alouds," a myriad of effective reading comprehension strategies (e.g., using text features, using text structures, summarizing, forming questions, monitoring comprehension), purposes for reading, and learning from reading. Teachers learn to integrate the relevant strategies that are within the text students are about to read. Teachers also learn cooperative learning strategies that support discussions of text with particular oral strategies (e.g., for recall, paraphrasing, summarization, question formulation, and sentence-starter frames). Teachers learn how to set up student pairs for paired reading and how to monitor for quality reading and application of comprehension strategies. Teachers also participate in teams of four in order to experience firsthand the management strategies that create effective cooperative contexts for learning.

Coaches and Administrators. By recording student responses during teacher "read-alouds," student partner reading, peer discussions, and cooperative learning activities, coaches and administrators can give specific feedback to teachers and students on the application of comprehension strategies.

Phase 3

Students. In Phase 3, students focus on text structures and writing conventions for differing purposes and apply them to a variety of subject-area writing tasks.

Teachers. Teachers learn how to highlight and discuss features of various types of text structures (e.g., expository, narrative, fable, persuasive). They also learn how to integrate writing strategies (e.g., identifying main ideas and author's purpose, connecting various parts of a text), editing activities and strategies (e.g., rewriting sentences, eliminating unnecessary repetitions, spelling, and grammar), and effective use of writing tools (e.g., outlines, concept maps, semantic maps, and graphic organizers) as they relate to different disciplines.

Coaches and Administrators. They learn how to record the complexities of teaching writing mechanics and processes in order to give precise feedback to teachers. Administrators also learn how to conduct constructive and robust teacher evaluations that continuously inform and improve teaching for ELs and other students.

Phase 4

Students. In Phase 4, students practice what they learned previously and learn the intricacies of oral discourse, communication skills, social and cooperative skills, and applying creativity.

Teachers. Teachers learn how to establish a context for the 21st-century skills (e.g., critical thinking, collaboration, communication, technology, problem solving, life and career skills such as flexibility and adaptability, initiative and self-direction, social and cross-cultural productivity and accountability, leadership and responsibility). Teachers use props and activities to help students practice effective communication (e.g., sentence and question starters, social protocols, instructions on how to interrupt politely, question, and reach consensus). Teachers learn a myriad of cooperative learning structures for different learning purposes. Teachers practice relinquishing control and empower students to become more creative in their learning and in the products and/or performances of that learning.

Coaches and Administrators. They learn to record effective discourse and interaction patterns that facilitate learning language, content concepts, and skills for the 21st century.

Phase 5

Students. In Phase 5, students learn to become autonomous learners and how to apply rigor in their learning.

Teachers. Teachers learn how to be efficacious in their instructional decisions. They also learn how to integrate all the strategies and activities from Phases 1 to 4 into their lessons. Teachers practice integrating vocabulary, reading, writing, and cooperative learning into whatever lesson design their school or district requires, or they integrate their skills into ready-made templates by ExC-ELL. Most important, teachers learn how important it is to give ELs and all other students more opportunities for oral displays of what they are reading and learning from that reading, more opportunities to write, and to offer choices and room for creativity.

Coaches and Administrators. They learn to help teachers fine-tune their lesson designs, set goals for subsequent observations, and analyze student performance.

School Improvement and School Reform

The ExC-ELL administrative sessions consist of what we call "Teacher Support Strategies" for administrators who (a) want to ensure success for their students by ensuring success for their teachers; (b) empower coaches whose role and goal are to facilitate continuous learning, fidelity of implementation, and quality instruction through effective feedback and support strategies; and (c) empower teachers working with their colleagues in Teacher Learning Communities.

Training of Trainers

After a successful year of implementation in schools, potential trainers emerge. These can be the on-site coaches or teacher leaders or classroom teachers who have become highly skilled in delivering the ExC-ELL instructional components. The potential trainers attend a three-day Trainer of Trainers (TOT) Institute where the ExC-ELL trainers model the training strategies, debrief, and have the participants practice each component. When they are comfortable with the training, participants are asked to cotrain with the ExC-ELL trainers in the next institute. Once they are certified, they can replicate the training at their school site.

Questions and Topics for Discussion

With your colleagues, rate the features of your current professional development instruction. Circle the number for each of the eight statements (10 is the highest score). Then, discuss your ratings, why they were rated that way, discrepancies, surprises, and then prioritize those that need immediate and long-term attention.

1. Professional development instruction is comprehensive since it addresses all categories of ELs and all other students in a cohesive systematic plan.

1	2	3	4	5	6	7	8	9	10

2. All our teachers attend professional development instruction related to ELs.

1	2	3	4	5	6	7	8	9	10

3. Our professional development instruction on ELs is held for 5 to 10 days each year.

1	2	3	4	5	6	7	8	9	10

4. Our professional development instruction on ELs includes three to five classroom observations and coaching for each teacher.

1	2	3	4	5	6	7	8	9	10

5. All our literacy, language, and content coaches attend all EL professional development sessions and spend additional days on coaching teachers with ELs.

1	2	3	4	5	6	7	8	9	10

6. All our administrators/coordinators/supervisors attend all professional development sessions and add days for learning/planning how to institute teacher support systems.

1	2	3	4	5	6	7	8	9	10

7. Our professional development instruction has specific language, literacy, and content outcomes for teachers and students.

1	2	3	4	5	6	7	8	9	10

8. We use a tested observation protocol to collect objective data on quality of implementation, teacher instructional progress, and student learning progress.

1	2	3	4	5	6	7	8	9	10

9. We have in place, with high implementation quality and fidelity, **10 features of school success and effective implementation** described earlier in this chapter.

1	2	3	4	5	6	7	8	9	10

10. Instruction in every classroom is high quality, rigorous, and appropriate for all of our ELs.

1	2	3	4	5	6	7	8	9	10

4 Instructional Program Options for ELs

Why have middle and high schools ELs, who were born, raised, and have attended schools in the United States, not achieved the academic proficiency to succeed in the all-English mainstream program? One important reason is that many EL programs offer watered-down curriculum or basic English instruction only. Thus, they do not prepare ELs for the rigorous, standards-based instruction in the mainstream classroom. Consequently, ELs learn only some "key" words, simplistic phrases and superficial concepts through mostly oral language, as opposed to the academic English that enables them to comprehend, speak, read, and write in the content areas.

After attending the typical ESL or SEI program, ELs are often mainstreamed into the regular English classrooms. There, the content area teachers discover that these students do not understand the words from the textbooks, do not comprehend what they are reading, struggle with advanced writing, and cannot express themselves orally. Most often, students are sent back to the program they attended before to learn basic English again. The vicious cycle is repeated, compounded by such factors as low self-esteem, apathy, absenteeism, and discipline problems.

How can we ensure that ELs not only become proficient in English but that they also have the content knowledge they need to succeed in school and in life? A variety of program options are available for school districts to implement as whole-school programs or as additions to the regular curriculum. The program options offer ELs bilingual or monolingual English instruction.

Programs that offer instruction in two languages include the following:

- Transitional Bilingual Education (TBE)
- Maintenance/Dual Language (DL)
- Two-Way Bilingual Instruction (TWBI)

Programs that instruct ELs in English include the following:

- Pull-out ESL/Bilingual
- Push-in ESL/Bilingual
- Structured English Immersion (SEI)
- English Immersion (EI)
- Sheltered English (SE)
- Integrated Language, Literacy, and Content Instruction by all mainstream teachers in middle and high schools

There are benefits and limitations for each program. Until we have more empirical data on all of them, we can only state that the ones that have shown positive outcomes are these: TWBI, DL, TBE, SEI, and Integrated Language, Literacy, and Content Instruction.

THE BEST PROGRAM OPTIONS TO HELP ELS

As described in Table 4.1, you have several options for selecting the type of program that best serves the needs of ELs at your school, the sequence of implementation, and the ways to organize the curriculum components. The process takes time as you explore all possibilities.

Before you make a decision, consider that ELs, like their English-speaking peers, are in dire need of effective academic, social, and cognitive skill development. They need a program of instruction that provides them with language and academic opportunities and experiences that will enable them to succeed in school. They need to be part of the global skills race in the country's economic competitiveness for this decade. The program you choose will teach ELs to integrate basic skills with content knowledge as well as think independently, solve problems, and make decisions.

Table 4.1 Type of ESL/Bilingual Programs

Type of Program	Key Features	Benefits or Drawbacks
Transitional Bilingual Education (TBE) in Quality TBE Students ✓ Learn the language of school. ✓ Learn the grade-level curriculum. ✓ Use English in real settings with native English speakers or English-dominant students. ✓ Have linguistic support when phasing in subjects one at a time. ✓ Use TBE in some programs for newcomers.	Children in K–6 classrooms receive instruction mainly in their home language with 30–45 minutes of instruction in ESL from K–3. At the end of third grade, they begin to transition into English instruction during the majority of the school day, until they are fully immersed in English at fourth or fifth grade.	**Benefits** Children feel more comfortable and accepted in schools. Their primary language is developed to a basic literacy level before transitioning into English instruction. **Drawbacks** Some programs keep the children in the home language too long or do not develop academic English by third grade to help ELs catch up with their peers. The consequences are that ELs always lag behind and become LT-ELs in secondary schools. The primary language also erodes after third grade. (High quality TBEs can limit these drawbacks.)
Maintenance/Dual Language (DL) in Quality Programs ✓ Develop strong academic skills and proficiency in both languages. ✓ Have lessons that are never repeated or translated in the other language, but concepts taught in one language are reinforced across the two languages in a spiraling curriculum, with concepts and knowledge building on each other.	They offer instruction in both languages from kindergarten through elementary school. In a few cases, the programs are also in middle and high school. The programs are mainly for ELs and native speakers of the same language.	**Benefits** Programs enable students to develop both their native and English languages to higher levels of proficiency and literacy skills. **Drawbacks** Programs require extensive administrative support and quality instruction in both languages, two critical features that many programs still lack. (High quality maintenance/DL programs can limit these drawbacks.)

(Continued)

Table 4.1 (Continued)		
Type of Program	*Key Features*	*Benefits or Drawbacks*
Two-Way Bilingual Instruction (TWBI) in Quality Programs ✓ Develop literate students who can function in two languages and two cultures. ✓ Include a philosophy shared by administrators, teachers, parents, and students.	K–12 classrooms include ELs and English native speakers who want to learn a second language such as Spanish. Most programs begin instruction in the minority language and add English each year until the third or fourth grade when both languages are allocated 50% of the time. The 50–50 version of this program offers instruction from K–12, allocating equal time to each language from kindergarten.	***Benefits*** All students become bilingual and biliterate and learn how to respect and interact with a different culture. Students in 50-50 programs are able to pass tests in English and the primary language by third grade. ***Drawbacks*** Programs require more resources, quality instruction in two languages, extensive collegial planning, and administrative and community support. Some programs have had success with only majority students, while others with only minority students, meaning that the instruction needs improvement.
Pull-Out ESL/Bilingual	This is typically offered in 30–40-minute blocks in elementary schools or whole periods in secondary schools. Students are pulled out of their classroom and grouped with one ESL teacher for basic oral English development.	***Benefits*** ELs have one teacher they can relate to and who can address their language and schooling needs. ***Drawbacks*** Some ESL/bilingual teachers have to work with multiple grade-level students in the same group. When ELs are pulled out of class, they miss valuable content and peer interaction. ELs fall behind in all subjects and do not develop English language and literacy.

Table 4.1		
Type of Program	Key Features	Benefits or Drawbacks
Push-In ESL/Bilingual	An ESL teacher goes into a classroom to work with one or a few students, mainly translating or facilitating understanding during instruction by the mainstream teacher.	**Benefits** The EL is present for the content and language of the mainstream classroom. This is potentially beneficial when there is one or a handful of ELs in a classroom. **Drawbacks** As EL populations grow, it becomes impossible for teachers to push in and address so many students. ELs fall behind in all subjects and do not develop English language and literacy.
Structured English Immersion (SEI)	This is implemented in elementary or secondary schools where teachers are highly skilled at teaching their mainstream curriculum with second language strategies to assist ELs learn content and English.	**Benefits** If teachers are well prepared, ELs move smoothly into English and are able to keep up with core subjects. **Drawbacks** Students' primary language erodes.
English Immersion (EI)	One or more ELs are immersed in English-only classrooms with teachers who are not certified/ credentialed or prepared to teach ELs.	**Benefits** Very few students are able to benefit from such immersion **Drawbacks** Students' primary language erodes. Students are rarely able to do well academically.

(Continued)

Table 4.1 (Continued)		
Type of Program	*Key Features*	*Benefits or Drawbacks*
Sheltered English (SE) ✓ Some programs for Newcomers use SE.	Programs are mainly implemented in secondary schools with teachers who are ESL credentialed and include some science or social studies or math curricula into their sheltered English blocks.	***Benefits*** ELs learn English and some content concepts, usually social studies. ***Drawbacks*** Sometimes the curriculum is watered down and simplified to an extreme. ELs need several sheltered courses in order to master English literacy and core content. This extends the time ELs need to graduate.
Integrated Language, Literacy, and Content Instruction ✓ Use language and literacy instruction that cuts across all content areas. ✓ Make literacy a priority among all teachers, staff, and administrators.	These are courses in secondary schools taught by mainstream teachers who have core subject credentials plus ESL certification or in-service training to teach language, literacy, and content in an integrated approach. This approach is also used in DL or TWBI. ExC-ELL is a model that has been empirically tested with significant results.	***Benefits*** Adolescent ELs learn English vocabulary, reading comprehension skills, and writing skills for each content area. ELs are able to catch up and keep up with their native-English peers. ***Drawbacks*** Mainstream teachers need extensive in-service training and follow-up coaching to help them integrate language and literacy development strategies into their content lessons and instructional strategies. School administrators are reluctant to invest time and resources to help all teachers in the school receive this preparation. (High quality Integrated Language, Literacy, and Content Instruction can limit these drawbacks.)

Your leadership role is crucial for the benefit of the ELs at your school. Research continues to indicate a strong correlation between school improvement and the leadership skills of administrators (DuFour, 2007). It points to leaders who do the following:

> Analyze the vision, mission, and core values of the school
> Align people to that vision and mission
> Build effective teams
> Create a climate for organizational change
> Gather and analyze data to make research-based goals
> Implement and monitor their plans to ensure success of their reform efforts (Hirsh, 2006; Kelly & Lezotte, 2003)

Without an administrator intrinsically involved in these changes but oriented toward ELs, the ultimate outcome of the reform will be jeopardized.

Planning Stage

The planning phase takes time. Fortunately, there are a number of successful programs with improved outcomes with websites for you and your staff to review before you make decisions. The School Improvement Plan can include the following steps for planning and designing a program option for the ELs at your school:

• Make a systemic commitment to ELs' education and improvement. Be upbeat: You are going to make great things happen in your school and move from good to great!
• Involve teachers, coaches, staff, administrators, even the surrounding community, to incorporate a quality program for ELs in the school offerings. Immerse yourself in real and positive change for the school. Involve your staff members in tasks that they can do well, and lead them away from the business-as-usual or old-way attitudes.
• Start by reviewing Table 4.1. Work on developing everyone's knowledge, skills, and dispositions in a concerted effort to grapple with the best program option for your students. Gather information on program options and discuss it in-depth. You are developing ownership and practicing shared ownership by involving all in the critical decisions.
• The chosen program is about change in support of equity and access to quality education: How can you sustain it? Take the fear out of change by others by assuming the responsibility to first try the program option selected.
• Most importantly, align your educational goals for ELs with those of all school students: How can you accomplish these goals for quality schooling for ELs and all students with high impact in a short time?

Making the Program Succeed

The program option has been selected, its design revised somewhat to fit the educational needs and characteristics of the targeted EL population. Although your selected program option has great potential to succeed, you, your staff, or the community have some concerns about its implementation. Numerous studies have been conducted and indicate some widespread tendencies that limit equal opportunities for ELs' academic success regardless of the program selected. We use them as a basis and recommend what would help sustain the effort and succeed.

Tips for Successful Program Implementation

1. Give the program option selected the same high status and resources as other programs.

2. Avoid program isolation from the mainstream program.

3. Provide sustained and ongoing quality professional development. Assist with teacher preparation to use research-based strategies to teach academic language and curriculum content.

4. Balance instructional time on oral language and literacy.

5. Focus on high levels of literacy.

6. Ensure that content language is preselected for instruction by level of use and function.

7. Persist no matter what. Resilience is on your side.

Those Who Teach ELs

The teachers you hire and train need to make a commitment to the vision and goals of the chosen program of instruction for ELs. Teacher quality is seen as an essential part of addressing student needs and reducing the achievement gap. Regardless of the program of instruction, research shows that teacher effectiveness connects to overall educational quality and has more impact on student achievement than other factors, such as class size (Liston, Borko, & Whitcomb, 2008).

Helping PreK–12 Teachers Qualify to Teach ELs

- Hire capable ESL, reading, bilingual teachers who can teach phonics, decoding, vocabulary, and reading comprehension along with academic domain language. They should have more than one ESL course or one literacy course in their repertoire.

- If incoming teachers lack the know-how to build on reading and writing skills in math, science, social studies, and language arts by integrating the components of oracy and literacy into their subject areas, provide the in-service support that is EL evidence-based to gain this know-how. Involve everyone and hold them accountable to jointly constructed EL literacy goals.
- Focus on professional development that integrates language, literacy, and subject matter knowledge for teaching ELs. Equip teachers to become literacy leaders. Ensure that professional development is sustained, coherent, comprehensive, and systematic in meeting the needs of all teachers.
- Align resources to ensure that efforts are suitably supported. The education of ELs may be expensive, burdensome, and time-consuming, but they and their teachers deserve the best!
- Create schedules to allow teacher teams to meet and discuss EL progress or lack of and to plan for immediate interventions and improvement.
- Ensure that resources are being well distributed and that ELs are benefitting from instruction in the program.

Questions and Topics for Discussion

1. What program option do you plan to implement and customize at your school to give ELs access to language development and challenging grade-level curriculum?
2. How do you plan to sustain the successful implementation of the selected program?
3. What are your plans to promote teacher effectiveness and growth?
4. What are the implications from this chapter for your school?
5. What would take these ideas to another level?

5 Selecting and Teaching Academic Vocabulary/ Discourse

This is the first of four chapters that covers characteristics of high quality instruction in depth. Vocabulary is the first important step toward school success for ELs and other students. They learn the words and use them in the classroom and in the content areas (science, math, history, literature). Past research and recent studies form the basic premises of the vocabulary instruction that has helped many ELs and struggling students accelerate their English learning and academic success (Calderón, 2007). Key messages from research inform us that

> Effective vocabulary instruction has to start early, in preschool, and continue throughout the school years (Nagy, 2005).
> Teaching vocabulary helps develop phonological awareness (Nagy, 2005) and reading comprehension (Beck, Perfetti, & McKeown, 1982).
> Vocabulary instruction needs to be explicitly taught before, during, and after reading to help ELs catch up with the words they are missing (Calderón, 2007; Calderón et al., 2005; Calderón & Minaya-Rowe, 2003; Hiebert & Kamil, 2005).
> ELs need discussions about word knowledge: cognates, affixes, pronunciation, decoding, multiple meanings, phrasal clusters, and idioms using the word in question (Calderón et al., 2009a; Grabe, 2009).

Activities That Do Not Help ELs

- Memorizing isolated lists of words or copying definitions and sentences from the board do not produce vocabulary growth.

- Drawing pictures of the word does not necessarily mean that a word will be used by the student.

SELECTING IMPORTANT WORDS FOR EACH CONTENT AREA

There is a wide range of language levels in every classroom. The heterogeneity in a school can also be attributed to age and grade-level spans, linguistic and cultural differences, learning disabilities, or differences in educational experiences. Since we cannot teach every word in the science, math, social studies, or language arts texts that ELs need to read every day, we must be selective and strategic about the words we select to teach.

Therefore, we want to select those words, phrases, statements, and questions starter that

- ✓ Are the most useful in learning the content and concepts students are about to read
- ✓ ELs need to use orally to describe, question, or summarize what they have learned
- ✓ ELs need to use in writing summaries, reports, and research papers

We can use the subsequent steps to select words to teach for any passage and any subject. Words to be selected come not only from textbooks but also from any text on computers or trade books.

Steps for Selecting Words to Teach

1. "Chunk" or parse the text into manageable parts.

2. Select language, reading comprehension, and core content standards, and language function, reading comprehension skill, and writing genre.

3. Select Tier 1, 2, and 3 words that are most useful to accomplish language, literacy, and content objectives.

Step 1. Parse the text. Peruse the text you are about to read aloud to your students or the text that students are about to read, whether for science, social studies, math, or language arts. If it contains too many words that might be unfamiliar, you might want to divide, or "chunk," it into smaller units. Next, proceed to underline the words your students absolutely must know to understand and learn this content. If it's a short story, poem, or novel chapter, select the words that are most important to the story grammar (e.g., plot, setting, and characterization). If it's a math, science, or social studies text, select the words that are most important in talking about that concept in academic language.

Step 2. Address standards. Think about the words that address core standards as well as language and literacy standards. For example, the WIDA guidelines recommend answering the following question: *What is the language ELs need to process or produce to describe, explain, compare, evaluate, identify, sequence, classify, categorize, predict, question, or match?* (Gottlieb, Cranley, Cammilleri, 2007). These discourse or oracy functions are basically the same as the reading comprehension strategies listed by most state reading standards. For example, "to describe" has some word and discourse formulas that can be used across the content areas—to talk about character motive or about a science experiment. The word/discourse formulas can be introduced and practiced during the preteaching of vocabulary. Thus, when selecting language functions, you are also selecting your reading comprehension strategies/skills and the writing structures your students will use to write about what they read. The integration of the language, reading, and writing strategies or skills becomes your objectives, aims, "can dos," or standards that you need to meet. This will facilitate the students' mastery of words and complex sentences that is required for them to do well on your test or the state exams. The following list contains some of the most often used strategies or functions.

Table 5.1	Language Functions, Reading Comprehension Strategies, and/or Writing Structures	
Describing	Defining	Enumerating
Classifying	Comparing/contrasting	Making inferences/hypotheses
Summarizing	Identifying	Interpreting
Explaining	Organizing	Retelling
Predicting	Asking and answering questions	Making connections
Visualizing	Monitoring comprehension	Determining important information
Sequencing	Finding problem solutions	Finding cause and effect

From Calderón, M., Carreón, A., Cantú, J., Minaya-Rowe, L. (2008, 2010).

It is interesting to note that linguists and second-language experts call these language functions, reading specialists call them reading skills or strategies, while writing experts refer to them as writing genre or writing mechanics. Whatever you choose to call them, they seem to be headed in the same direction. They serve to help students express themselves academically in oral or written texts and to comprehend the texts that generate those verbal and written functions.

Step 3. Categorize words before the final selection. From the words or clusters of words that you have underlined, categorize them into three tiers, selecting no more than five or six for each tier. If you have considerably more than that, the text may be too difficult for your students. It will take too long to teach all those words and the comprehension will be stifled at best. If there are many more words that your ELs might need, that is an indicator that they may need a special intervention from an ESL teacher who can preteach those words. If you don't have enough words, the text is too easy or doesn't have enough conceptual substance.

USING WORD CATEGORIES

Tier 3 Words. It is easier to begin selecting words or units of meaning (clusters such as ice ages, prime numbers, stimulus package) from Tier 3. These are words that are subject-specific. Typically, grade-level trade books and textbooks highlight in bold the Tier 3 words and include them in a glossary as the most important words. These words tell us immediately what discipline is being studied, as we see in this example.

Table 5.2	Sample Tier 3 Words		
Math	*Science*	*Social Studies*	*Language Arts*
Rectangle	Germ	Government	Personification
Denominator	Atom	Bylaws	Shifty character
Balanced equation	Osmosis	Congressional districts	Cause and effect
Pi square	Matter	Capital	Inference
To the nth power	Power surge	Power of attorney	Powerful potion
Divide	Cell division	Divide and conquer	Divisive

About 40% of Tier 3 words are cognates with Latin-derived languages such as Spanish, French, and Italian. **Cognates** are words that sound, are spelled, and have similar meanings across languages. See the following table, for example:

Cognates	
English words	*Spanish words*
denominator	denominador
congress	congreso
cause and effect	causa y efecto
personification	personificación
osmosis	osmosis
radical	radical

Tier 2 Words. Tier 2 words may be the most ignored when it comes to vocabulary instruction. The Tier 2 category includes phrasal clusters, idioms, polysemous (multiple meaning) words, processing words, connectors, sophisticated words, and words to provide specificity to describe a concept. These are the words that nest the Tier 3 words. They hold together or glue the meaning of a complex word.

Tier 1 Words. These are simple words known by virtually all mainstream students within an age group, but not necessarily by ELs.

Table 5.3 Sample Tier 2 Words	
Phrasal clusters	stored energy, skim through, run your hand over, stimulus package, over the course of
Idioms, social function words, clusters	Break a leg. It's over his head. I'm just looking. I'm good. I know what you mean. If … then …. The problem is solved by ….
Polysemous	trunk, power, cell, left, right, light, prime
Processing	apparent, assortment, assumption, basis, crucial, device, display, illustrate, generate, effect, affect, allow
Connectors	subsequently, although, as well as, however, as a result of, in order to, in contrast, for instance
Sophisticated/specificity	shuddered, scrutiny, celestial, wholesome

Source: Calderón, M., Carreón, A., Cantú, J., & Minaya-Rowe, L. (2010). *Expediting comprehension for English language learners: Participants' manual.* New York: Benchmark Education Company.

They may not have the background knowledge for the concept, may not recognize the spelling or the pronunciation, or may not recognize the cognate or false cognate. Although Tier 1 words are the easiest words in a text, they are the hardest to identify for instruction because we may not be able to guess ahead of time which ones a particular EL or ELs know or need. Begin by selecting those you think they will need. Then, as you observe and listen to the ELs conduct their partner reading and discussions on what they read, you will be able to identify other words they need.

Table 5.4 Sample Tier 1 Words	
Spelling	tough, phrase, highlight, toothache
Pronunciation	sell/cell, axis/exes, ship/chip
Background knowledge	skyscraper, lawnmower, blender, parka
False cognate	embarrassed, exit, success, character

Source: Calderón, M., Carreón, A., Cantú, J., & Minaya-Rowe, L. (2010). *Expediting comprehension for English language learners: Participants' manual.* New York: Benchmark Education Company.

TEACHING VOCABULARY BEFORE READING

All students need explicit and varied instruction to build word power. Teaching vocabulary should be pervasive throughout the school in order to instill in students the essence of semantic awareness— the mindset that they should be learning words every period of the day. Therefore, all teachers in the school need to commit to systematic vocabulary instruction.

A seven-step process for introducing the most important and most complex words or clusters of words is used at the beginning of a lesson, before a teacher read-aloud or before students are to read a text. The Tier 1 to 3 words can be taught as a whole-class or small group process. The teachers use chart paper, blackboards, PowerPoint presentations, or whiteboards to present the seven steps. It is important that the students see the seven steps written out. These include the word, the sentence as they will encounter it later on during reading, the dictionary definition, a student friendly cue, some grammatical or phonological aspects of a difficult word, and the activity for Step 6. The seven-step process lends itself best for teaching Tier 2 and 3 words because those are more sophisticated and complex. A simplified version for teaching Tier 1 is described after the seven steps.

Seven-Step Process for Tier 2 and 3 Words

A PowerPoint slide might look like Table 5.5. Teachers use the seven-step template on the left to remember to address the seven steps.

Table 5.5 Example of Seven Steps	
1. Teacher states the word in context from the text.	1. Weather can have a big *effect* on your life.
2. Teacher asks students to repeat the word three times.	2. Say *effect* three times with me and three more times whispering it.
3. Teacher provides the dictionary definition(s).	3. The definition is "the result or consequence of something. "
4. Teacher explains the meaning with student-friendly definitions.	4. Windy days have a big, negative, *effect* on my allergies.
5. Teacher highlights features of the word: polysemous, cognate, tense, prefixes, etc.	5. Notice how we spell *effect*. Spell it with me. What is its cognate in Spanish?
6. Teacher engages students in activities to develop word/concept knowledge.	6. What has had a big *effect* on your grades recently? Tell your buddy and use *effect* several times as you share. After a minute ask the following: Who wants to tell me what your buddy said?
7. Teacher reminds students how this will be used after reading.	7. Remember to use this word in your Exit Pass today as you summarize what you read.

1. The teacher reads and shows the word in the sentence (context) from the text. This helps students remember the word in context when they begin to read and to grasp the meaning.

2. The students repeat the word several times with and without the teacher to practice pronunciation.

3. The teacher provides the dictionary or glossary definition(s). This is exposure to formal English and what students themselves will encounter later when they are proficient enough in English to use a dictionary.

4. The teacher explains the meaning with student-friendly definitions or gives an example that students can relate to. The teacher uses simple language, familiar examples, pictures, props, movement, and gestures to help students comprehend the meaning or in some cases multiple meanings.

5. The teacher highlights an aspect of the word that might create difficulty: spelling, multiple meanings, cognates/false cognates, prefixes, suffixes, base words, synonyms, antonyms, homophones, grammatical variations, and so forth. Students will do more in-depth word study on what was highlighted later on. The preteaching steps should be the opportunity for oral production on meaning and exposure to the written word in context. Steps 1 to 6 should move quickly so that no more than two or three minutes per word or 10 to 15 minutes for all the words are spent in preteaching key vocabulary. We want to make sure to leave plenty of time for us to model reading strategies, for students to read, verbally summarize, and write.

6. The teacher engages 100% of the students in ways to orally use/own the word and concept (e.g., TPS = Think-Pair-Share; Turn to your partner and share how . . . ; Who wants to tell me what your partner said?; Which do you prefer . . . ? Answer in a complete sentence). **Writing the word, drawing, or other word activities should come later after reading**. First, students need to use the word orally, several times in a variety of ways.

7. The teacher assigns peer reading with oral and written summarization activities and how the new words need to be used or how students will be accountable for these words.

For younger children in preschool through first grade, we use a shorter version with five steps:

Five-Step Vocabulary Process for PreK–1 ELs

1. Introduce the new word in a natural setting and use concrete objects.

2. Explain the word using everyday language. Provide a child-friendly definition.

3. Give examples of the word in a variety of contexts. Use complete sentences.

Things to Remember for Preteaching Vocabulary

1. ELs need to produce the word 10 to 12 times orally during the preteaching segment.

2. Step 6 is the most important.

3. Spend 12 to 15 minutes at the beginning of each class teaching vocabulary.

4. Post the tiers as reminders to use these words.

---

4. Ask children to say a sentence to their buddy or invent another with the new word. Ask them to share their sentences.

5. Continue using the word at every opportunity—at home and at centers. Acknowledge the children's attempts at using the new word(s).

Teaching Tier 1 Words

Most Tier 1 words will be concrete words and those can be demonstrated easily through visuals, motions, and gestures. The whiteboards facilitate quick drawings and photos from the Internet. Any ESL strategies typically used by ESL teachers can be used to teach Tier 1 words, as long as the activities do not last more than two minutes. We often see students taking 5 to even 10 minutes with one word as they copy sentences from the board, look up words in dictionaries, and draw pictures—silently. These are time-fillers but not vocabulary teaching/learning activities.

Explicit Instruction for Tier 2 Words

Teaching Polysemous Words. The seven steps can be used to teach words that have multiple meanings (polysemous words) while introducing two or three meanings, but the teacher should always emphasize the meaning as used in the text students are about to read. Most students will be familiar with four or more meanings of words like *trunk* (e.g., back of a car, tree trunk, body trunk, elephant trunk, large suit case), but not necessarily the ELs. In such cases, ask students who know a meaning to role-play it and have the students ask the class to say the word three times.

Teaching Long Phrases. Idioms, noun phrases, and prepositional phrases need to be taught as a whole chunk or clusters. For example, *on the spur of the moment, break a leg, from one day to the next, at the turn of the century, as well as,* are easier learned when the whole term is presented and practiced.

Table 5.6 Sentence Starters for Different Language Functions	
Verbal functions, reading comprehension strategies, and/or writing text structures	*Sample sentence starters*
To describe cause and effect	because, due to, as a result, since, for this reason, therefore, in order to, so that, thus
To compare and/or contrast	and, also, as well as, in addition, likewise, moreover, by the way, or, but, although, however, in contrast, whereas, nevertheless, on the other hand, while, on the contrary, by comparison, ironically, yet, even though, just as … so
To give examples	for example, for instance, in particular, such as, in this situation, to illustrate, to demonstrate, in fact, indeed, in this case
To describe a sequence	First … second…, subsequently, following this, next, finally, concurrently, additionally, meanwhile
To bring to conclusion or describe results	in conclusion, ultimately, as a result, finally, thus, therefore, hence, accordingly, as we have seen, as we have shown, this led to, in essence
Polite discussions	apparently, probably, likely, might, rarely, seldom, at times, sometimes, occasionally, theoretically, on the one hand, on the other hand

Source: Calderón, M., Carreón, A., Cantú, J., & Minaya-Rowe, L. (2010). *Expediting comprehension for English language learners: Participants' manual.* New York: Benchmark Education Company.

Teaching Connectors and Compound Sentences. For students to write cohesive paragraphs and use compound sentences or more complex syntax, they need explicit instruction on transition words such as *because, and, then, next, but, however.* Connectors and transition words not only help oral expression but also to write cohesively. Some examples of connectors for different functions of language, reading comprehension strategies, and targeted writing are shown in Table 5.6.

These charts are given to students to use during discussions or when constructing questions or during writing. Teachers give them as laminated handouts to students to keep in their desks for continuous use. Some teachers glue them on folder tents placed at the center of the tables during student discussions. Others hang them with yarn from the ceiling directly at the students' eye level or simply post them on chart paper throughout the classroom.

TEACHING SPECIFICITY AND SOPHISTICATED WORDS

Tier 3 words are not the only "sophisticated" or difficult words, as we have seen. Many Tier 2 words are just as complex. For example, *accuracy, additive, crucial, depict, deplete* are Tier 2 words that are found in most state exams. If ELs are to do well on those tests, it behooves us to teach as many of those rich words, along with more refined adjectives and adverbs. One reason why LT-ELs do not move from one level of English proficiency to another quickly enough is that rich words are not being taught or practiced.

TEACHING COGNATES AND FALSE COGNATES

Cognates are words in English and Spanish or other languages that look alike and have same meanings. When pointed out explicitly, cognates help students comprehend many content-specific words. Cognates also help students do better in spelling in English! They learn to compare and contrast and remember the differences. Teachers always ask, "But what about the other languages that don't have cognates? Is it fair to point out cognates in Spanish and not in the others? Yes. Just keep in mind that you will be helping Spanish speakers, and other students will also benefit from comparing and contrasting. These students will benefit from the metalinguistic analyses. It will make them more "language aware." Their English-speaking peers probably already have learned some words in Spanish and will welcome others. Be sure to pronounce them because the pronunciation usually varies. Some examples are as follows:

English words	Spanish words
control	control
algebra	algebra
osmosis	osmosis
onomatopoeia	onomatopeya

Spelling differences between cognates have patterns (such as the ones in Table 5.7) that help ELs predict and remember the correct form in English.

Table 5.7	Spelling Differences Between English and Spanish Cognates		
Nouns	*Adjectives*	*Verbs*	*Adverbs*
-ion = ión	-ous = -oso	-ate = -ar	-ly = -mente
action/acción	curious/curioso	decorate/decorar	absolutely/absolutamente

Table 5.8	Helpful Word Patterns		
Nouns	*Adjectives*	*Verbs*	*Adverbs*
alphabet	alphabetic	alphabetize	alphabetically
alfabeto	alfabético	alfabetizar	alfabéticamente
favor	favorable	favor	favorably
favor	favorable	favorecer	favorablemente

Comparing word roots and affixes also helps students with spelling and meaning. Some basic patterns are shown in Table 5.8.

Bilingual teachers should also point out *false cognates*—words that do not mean the same in English and Spanish, although they look and sound similar. See the following, for example:

> Exit is not éxito, which means success, and success is not suceso, which means happening or event.
> Library is not librería; it is a biblioteca.
> If character refers to disposition or moral values and personality, then its cognate is character, but personaje is the character in a story or play.
> Consentir means to "consent" but also to spoil or pamper people.
> Masa means mass (indefinite matter or group of people) but also dough for bread or for tortillas. Mass (religious ceremony) is misa in Spanish.

There are Tier 2 sophisticated words that are more commonplace in Spanish and that native speakers will readily recognize such as *docile, domicile,* and *dental.*

Grammar/Syntax

The seven-step vocabulary strategy also highlights grammar, pronunciation, and spelling. Some examples of grammatical structures that can be taught from the context of what they are about to read are compound sentences, passive voice sentences, connectors, and prepositional phrases.

Compound sentences are chunks of words that contain long noun phrases such as the following: *If our students are to succeed, then it is imperative that we teach complex sentence structures, punctuation markers, phrases, and words that connect those long sentences.* When passive voice or the voice of science is added, it can complicate meaning for ELs. See the following, for example: *Before division can occur, the genomic information which is stored in chromosomes must be replicated and the duplicated genome separated cleanly between cells.* Examples of connectors or prepositional phrases that help sentence cohesion are these: *next, besides, is __ than __, if . . . then . . . , since, nevertheless, in spite of, according to . . . .*

TEACHING VOCABULARY DURING READING

Vocabulary can be taught during reading. It can be taught during teacher read-alouds, or students can use strategies that the teacher models while reading the first paragraph of the assigned text. There are several "meaning-making" strategies and "fix-it" strategies that help students understand a word. If these fail, the students can write it on a sticky note and put it in the "Parking Lot" (discussed later) or in a "Word Box." The next chapter describes how strategic reading can be applied to vocabulary development as well as reading comprehension.

TEACHING AND ASSESSING VOCABULARY ON-THE-RUN

Vocabulary on-the-run. Walk around with a notepad or the EOP and listen to the students read and discuss what they read. Make note of the Tier 1, 2, or 3 words they use. If a word is not used appropriately, teach it right there on the spot. We call this "teaching words on-the-run" because you provide the meaning and examples during the instant that you know a student needs your help with a word. Be sure to ask the student to give you a sentence with that word on the spot, too.

Sticky Notes and Parking Lots. Another strategy is to give sticky notes to the students, ask them to write a word on each that they still have trouble understanding and to hand these to you as you walk by. Remind them to first attempt to understand a word by discussing it with their buddy or looking it up in the glossary or dictionary. This is also a great assessment tool that tells you on a daily basis which words need reteaching or elaboration. Some teachers have a poster on a wall called a "Parking Lot" where the students can put the sticky notes for you. You can teach them after the reading activity, interrupt them, or wait until the next day to teach these words.

Student Word Banks. This type of note taking during reading helps ELs keep track of unfamiliar words. ELs can keep these words as journal entries, in learning logs, vocabulary banks, or cards on a ring that will serve as personal dictionaries. They make note of a word in the first column and write what they think it means in the second. After reading, they go to a dictionary or consult others to write the appropriate meaning. Here is one example:

New Word for Me	Maybe it Means . . .	Yes! This Is What It Means.

Attempt the Context. After teaching key Tier 1, 2, and 3 words, do a think-aloud to model strategies for learning words from context. While reading in pairs, the buddies can try these steps when they encounter a difficult word or a sentence that does not make sense. Once the strategy is internalized and is working, individual students can also apply this reflection process. The steps can be written on bookmarkers:

Attempt the Context

Step 1: Ask, What is the word that doesn't make sense in the sentence?

Step 2: Read the sentence again, and the one before, and the one after.

Step 3: Change the word to an easy word you know. Does the sentence make sense now?

Step 4: If still not sure, write the word in your learning log or on a sticky note.

VOCABULARY LEARNING AFTER READING

Using semantic maps, webs, diagrams, or any cognitive (graphic) organizer helps students anchor the new vocabulary and concepts. It also gives ELs more vocabulary for talking about new knowledge or new words. First, the teacher models on the board techniques for mapping. Second, small groups of students work on their maps. This preliminary practice provides ELs patterns to replicate. Encourage students to use drawings for those words not yet in their repertoire.

By classifying or reclassifying, not just vocabulary but also concepts into meaningful units, it will make new words easier to remember. Students in pairs or teams can group words according to the following:

- Nouns, adjective, or verbs
- Topics (words about *plants, communities*)
- Practical function (parts of the computer; joining words)
- Linguistic function (words for requesting, apologizing, demanding, denying)
- Dissimilarity or opposition (friendly/unfriendly; dangerous/safe)

New words or clusters can be written on color-coded cards or foldables (three-dimensional organizers such as booklets, trifolds, four-door, isosceles triangles, volcano shape, and other examples for math, science, social studies, and language arts). These cards or foldables can also become the word bank of the student. They can be used for peer-learning activities where students drill each other for meaning, concept mastery, or spelling. These cards can also be kept in envelopes or on a ring or hung on strings from the ceiling for easy consultation during writing activities.

DEBRIEFING OR METALINGUISTIC AND METACOGNITIVE PROCESSING

Once a strategy for making meaning of a word is chosen, whether through explicit instruction, think-alouds, buddy-buzz around a word, attempting contextual clues, or any other strategy, it is important to follow up with debriefing of learning. Debriefing helps develop metalinguistic and metacognitive skills. It helps students become **semantically aware**. That is, students become more in tune and sensitive to the way they approach words and what works for them in learning those words.

Semantic Awareness

- Semantic awareness is a cognitive, metacognitive, affective, and linguistic stance toward words.

- It is a mindset that word consciousness involves motivating and showing students how important it is to be learning words.

- Students who are word conscious are aware of the power of words they read, hear, write, and speak.

- Semantic awareness helps students become more skillful and precise in word usage at many levels of complexity and sophistication (Calderón, 2009).

Teach the concept of *semantic awareness*, then proceed with the debriefing by asking students questions such as these:

- What helped you remember a word?
- What will help you not to forget its meaning?
- How did you and your partner help each other when you didn't know a word?
- Who wants to share another **semantic strategy**?

Cooperative Learning for Debriefing

Buddy Buzz. Ask partners to discuss one of the answers before you call on one of them. Or, have a team of four "put their heads together" and talk about the strategies they used and which worked better. Ask one student to tell you which ones worked and another student to tell you where they had problems.

Corners for Words. At the end of the reading segment, even before you start a question-and-answer segment, conduct a "Corners" or "Go to the Wall" activity. *Corners* is where students are asked to go to the four corners of the room and talk about the words that were introduced that day. *Go to the Wall* is where students go stand along the wall in triads and each has 30 seconds to tell the other two how many words he remembers from the reading and preteaching of vocabulary.

Questions and Topics for Discussion

1. Why is vocabulary/discourse important?
2. How can we incorporate more vocabulary instruction into our daily routines?
3. What are some ways to promote semantic awareness throughout our school?
4. Why spend only 12 to 15 minutes preteaching vocabulary?
5. What are some activities that we can conduct in our Teacher Learning Communities to ensure quality teaching of vocabulary?

6 Reading in the Content Areas

The National Reading Panel (2000) has identified five components for all students, including ELs, to become good readers: phonemic awareness, phonics, fluency, vocabulary, and reading comprehension. ELs need these components to recognize words and comprehend a text at the same time. They also need extra time and quality activities for vocabulary and academic language development. For ELs, recognizing vocabulary does not only mean reading words aloud but also learning their meanings. ELs need to comprehend at least 85% to 90% of the words in a sentence, a question, a paragraph, or any text.

OBSTACLES TO OVERCOME IN HELPING ELS

- Using reading instructional strategies that were developed and tested *only* for mainstream students.
- Rushing to get ELs on the same page as mainstream students; the results are pushbacks for them *and* also for the mainstream students.
- Assuming that ELs are fluent readers because they can read a number of words in one minute. ELs may decode as quickly as possible in attempts to please you, but they may not comprehend a word they are reading.
- Focusing on speed to improve automaticity and reading fluency rather than comprehension. There is no such thing as a scientifically based approach to speed reading.

These practices are detrimental for ELs. They only help them to fall further and further behind in developing academic vocabulary and reading comprehension skills. Content reading will continue to present difficulties. ELs will lose the motivation to read and become the struggling readers reading below several grade levels, and they still will be limited in their English proficiency. They will become the reluctant, apathetic learners in our classrooms and potential dropouts.

HELPING STUDENTS

The good news is that recent advances in EL literacy have begun to point us in the right direction (Calderón, 2009; RAND, 2002). The following practices can be incorporated in your daily teaching.

Effective Literacy Teaching

☐ Teach vocabulary and grammar in the context of what students are about to read.

☐ Teach phonics and phonological awareness for students to recognize the words only as needed for older students and also in the context they are reading.

☐ Incorporate academic concepts and content using students' background knowledge and vocabulary knowledge.

☐ Teach strategies for reading comprehension together in the context of the text students are about to read.

☐ Use your students' strengths, interests, and experiences to build the academic rigor and help them succeed.

☐ Teach your students to comprehend text features and genre such as nonfiction (e.g., newspapers, Internet texts, and subject matter textbooks) and fiction (e.g., readers' theater, fairy tales, fables, plays, and poems).

Incorporating Reading for ELs Into a School Improvement Plan

In order to succeed in school, ELs need a full range of reading skills, different types and levels of vocabulary, fluency, and mastery of the concepts/content they are reading (Calderón, 2007). The following five suggested steps for language and literacy development can be sequential or overlapping and part of the School Improvement Plan (SIP):

Step 1. Teachers select words to teach according to ELs' language and reading levels. The words range from easy to sophisticated to content-specific, concept-laden words. They orchestrate vocabulary learning and practice, discourse and word analysis activities before, during, and after reading. They teach grammar knowledge to support reading.

Step 2. Teachers introduce ELs to basic reading (and basic decoding skills if needed) and reading strategies that support comprehension. They model through think-alouds effective reading comprehension strategies: for example, text features, text structures, summarizing, forming questions, monitoring comprehension. Students work in pairs and in groups and the teacher monitors for quality reading, use of new vocabulary, and oral strategies, like recall, summarization, question formulation, and sentence starter frames.

Step 3. Teachers highlight and discuss features of various types of text structures and writing for different purposes (e.g., reporting, descriptive, narrative, persuasive/argumentative). They ask students to integrate content words within explicitly taught writing strategies (e.g., identifying main ideas, connecting various parts of a text), editing activities and strategies (e.g., rewriting sentences, eliminating unnecessary repetitions, spelling, grammar), and writing tools (e.g., outlines, concept maps, semantic maps, graphic organizers).

Step 4. Teachers use prompts and cooperative learning activities to help students practice effective communication (e.g., sentence and question starters, social protocols, instruction on how to politely interrupt, question, reach consensus, debate, etc.) and to monitor their progress.

Step 5. Teachers give students opportunities for inquiry and creativity as they become autonomous learners, apply rigor in their learning, and do more self-monitoring.

Higher Order Reading Processes

We teach comprehension strategies for students to relate ideas in a text to what they already know and make explicit what they don't know, to keep track of how well they understand what they read, and, when they don't, to identify what is causing the problem and how to solve it. Strategy instruction is very important for ELs. It helps them make it in a schooling system that is new to them. They figure out the simplest book conventions and concepts of print to applying the more sophisticated strategies of selecting key information, organizing and mentally summarizing information, monitoring comprehension, and matching comprehension to teacher goals or test goals.

A word of caution: ELs *cannot* be expected to make predictions or inferences or visualize if they don't know the words to understand or to express that prediction or inference or to form mind-movies. They may also have difficulty making connections to certain prior knowledge that is not part of their culture or schooling experiences (Calderón, 2009).

For Beginning ELs

> Start with asking and answering questions, determining important information, summarizing, making connections/use of schema, and monitoring comprehension.
> Give ELs the opportunity to apply a strategy immediately with math, science, social studies, as well as language arts, which reinforces the knowledge of the strategy and gives teachers an opportunity to check the appropriate use of those strategies when they practice with peers.

Sentence Starters for Oral and Written Discourse for Beginning ELs

Summarizing—ELs create a new text that stands for an existing text. The summary contains the important information in the text. They retell the big ideas, important facts, or information.

- This story tells about a . . .
- This section is about the . . .
- One important fact here is that . . .

Determining Important Information—ELs identify the most important idea in a section of text. They distinguish the important idea from details that tell more about it.

- The main idea is . . .
- The key details that support that are . . .
- The purpose of this text is to . . .

Monitoring Comprehension—ELs evaluate text understanding and use fix-it strategies to fix comprehension difficulties.

- I don't understand this sentence. I had better read it again.
- I don't understand this sentence. Which word is new for me? Do I know a word in Spanish that fits here?
- I don't understand this long sentence. I'm going to break it up.

Asking and Answering Questions—ELs create relevant questions to guide their reading for explicit and implicit text information. They use prior knowledge and information in the text to ask and answer questions.

- What is this text about?
- What do I already know about this topic?
- What do I want to know or need to know about this?
- What did the teachers say was our objective?

Sequencing—ELs make sense of the order in which ideas are presented to enhance comprehension.

- The first step in this experiment is . . .
- The sequence for answering this math problem is . . .
- The first thing the character did was to . . . . Next, the character . . .

Making Connections/Visualizing/Creating Schema—ELs practice relating new information with prior knowledge from their own culture or schooling. They create images to make connections between texts and their own lives and the world. They create images using all their senses and from their emotions to understand what they are reading. They create schema when teachers model a variety of these strategies.

- This reminds me of the time when I . . .
- My parents told me a story . . .
- I read in another book that . . .

Reminder

1. Handle strategy instruction with care and do not make it too complicated. Manage your time so that ELs do not spend too much time thinking about the strategy.

2. Make mastery of content the priority. Your goal is for ELs to get meaning from the reading selection and focus on the texts.

3. ELs benefit from explicit explanations of some key strategies for finding **cause and effect, comparison and contrast,** and **problem-solution**.

Sentence Starters for Strategy Application for ELs

Cause and effect

As a result of . . .
The cause was . . . and the effect was . . .
So that . . .

Comparison and contrast

This one has 2 feet and that one has 4.
Both are the same because . . .
They are different because . . .

Problem-Solution

The problem was that . . . and the solution was . . .
The problem could be that . . .
I think the answer is . . .

Preparing to Teach Reading and the Contents of Any Text

Think data-based instruction. What formal and informal measures can I use to assess students' comprehension? Analyze ELs' work so that instruction can be geared to their levels of language and/or reading stages. Monitor progress so that the instructional program can be revised if students are not making adequate progress. ELs need to read across texts to build understanding of big ideas. Have on hand collections of different sources of information through different genres. Select materials to build essential information and also be of interest to the ELs. Once you have a text in mind, consider the following:

1. What is the standard you are trying to meet?

2. Determine desired outcomes for oracy, reading, and writing skills. How will you convey these to the ELs?

3. Identify the potential in texts for various instructional purposes.

   o Kinds of challenges a text would present to ELs—reading levels, comprehension, cultural context.
   o Select text that provides potential for particular instructional purposes and can be handled by ELs.

4. Decide which vocabulary words to preteach so that ELs can understand and participate in the discussions, answer questions, and comprehend what they are about to read.

5. Select questions for discussions.

6. Select ancillary materials to ensure comprehension of big ideas: real objects, pictures, websites, role plays, gestures, drawings.

7. Select reading comprehension or metacognitive strategy to model for the students and plan how to model it.

8. Select appropriate strategy to use in helping students produce writing.

9. Differentiate level of scaffolding to provide different levels of support.

10. Determine desired outcomes for oracy, reading, and writing skills and how you will assess these.

Process for Teaching Reading Comprehension

Your first step was building comprehension; you pretaught the words for students to derive meaning from the text. For reading comprehension, the natural sequence is as follows:

1. Model how to deconstruct each sentence, with a student, in order to construct meaning.

2. Read aloud and think aloud to model a comprehension strategy.

3. Ask students to apply the deconstruction strategy and the comprehension strategy.

4. Model how to summarize what they have learned after each paragraph using the new words in their summaries.

5. Have students read with their buddies, alternating sentences, and summarize after each paragraph.

6. Monitor students by walking around the classroom, recording students' use of strategies as they conduct partner reading.

Example of the Teacher Modeling Process

Begin by modeling how to **deconstruct a sentence in order to construct meaning** and to identify words that still need clarifying. Use the following passage as a sample; the text in bold and brackets illustrates your think-aloud for monitoring comprehension.

> **It's a blustery January day** {a really cold January day} **in New York's Central Park. Squirrels dig through the snow-covered ground in search of acorns buried months ago** {the squirrels are digging in the snow looking for acorns they buried when there was no snow}. **Your friends are eager** {excited and they want you to hurry up} **for you to put on your ice skates and join them on the frozen pond** {they want to ice skate; here's a picture of ice skating in Central Park}. **The temperature must be at least 5°C less than yesterday** {What is that "C"? Is it centigrade; is it centimeter? I'm not sure. My reading partner isn't sure either. I had better ask my teacher. I'm going to put this on a sticky note and put the sticky note on the PARKING LOT so that my teacher can explain this to us}.

Substitute some of the words for easier words. Simplifying the language helps students see how they can also do their think-alouds with easy words. Showing students that "we don't know everything and that we ask after we've tried figuring it out" is a way of reassuring our students that it is all right to get help. After you model, ask students to read a paragraph with their reading buddy and deconstruct it sentence by sentence to make sure they understand what they are reading.

Teacher Modeling: A Comprehension Strategy

On Day 2, conduct think-alouds to model comprehension strategies such as *summarizing*, finding *cause and effect* or the *main idea*, or *sequencing*. See the following, for example:

- Read a paragraph aloud and then summarize at the end.
- Alternatively, with the help of another student, model how to read alternating sentences and summarize at the end of each paragraph.
- Emphasize that this time, instead of deconstructing, they are actually constructing quality sentences using as many of the new words as possible.
- Remind them of this: "You are activating your working memory that has all the new words."

Partner Reading

After you model with a student, ELs need to practice a strategy immediately with a partner. Partner reading and summarizing is critically important for ELs while reading math, science, and social studies. Ten minutes of daily partner reading reinforces the knowledge of the strategy and helps students understand and learn the content areas. The most effective partner reading approaches are these:

- Students alternate reading sentences aloud with a partner.
- The first student reads a sentence and does a think-aloud, followed by the second student who reads the next sentence and also does a think-aloud.
- Pairs alternate reading each sentence aloud (without the think-aloud), followed by both pairs talking about what they read after each paragraph.

Another option is just to ask students to read a paragraph while alternating sentences (without the think-alouds) and then summarize what they read at the end of each paragraph.

Why Read Only One Sentence at a Time?

- Students are more confident as they approach reading in smaller chunks.

- Both partners are on task. There is no time for distraction as they have to listen to each other.

- They have to retell (summarize) what they read after each paragraph.

How Do I Monitor Partner Reading?

- While students are partner reading, walk from pair to pair and catch them doing something right!
- Record a strategy used, application of new words, fluency, or extended discourse.
- Give feedback to the students or share their monthly progress with the parents.

Cooperative Learning Helps to Learn the Content

- Students can work in pairs, triads, or fours while they practice their new language and reading skills in safe contexts with peers.

- Most language, literacy, and information processing activities lend themselves to cooperative learning.

- There are many cooperative learning strategies and methods for developing vocabulary, reading, and writing.

Chapter 8 gives examples of cooperative learning strategies that are used after reading to anchor knowledge, review for exams, or give opportunities for inquiry and creativity.

Writing for Anchoring Reading and Vocabulary

The final element in the sequence of language and reading is writing about what is being learned every day and producing a summative piece at the end of the week or the unit. Small pieces of writing related to what students are reading can be introduced at the end of the lesson or before transitioning to a different subject, leaving 5 to 10 minutes for students to write a few lines on their **Exit Pass**. Exit Passes are usually one quarter of a standard-size page that teachers distribute for daily use. Assignments for Exit Passes can be as simple as "Write two or three sentences about what you read and learned today" or "Write five new, sophisticated words you learned." A simple blank Exit Pass suffices.

Exit Pass For

Name _____ Date _____

_____

_____

_____

_____

When the bell rings, students bring up the Exit Pass as they leave the room or when they get ready for the next subject area. Other activities for anchoring knowledge, vocabulary, and grammar are presented in the following chapters.

Questions and Topics for Discussion

1. How many of our students read one or two levels below their grade level?
2. How many read three or more levels below their grade level?
3. How many need tutoring or another immediate intervention?
4. What type of reading intervention do they need? Is it more academic vocabulary?
5. Is it basic decoding with meaningful words and texts? Is it reading comprehension strategies?
6. How many students fall into each of those categories?
7. How can we ensure that all our teachers are teaching/modeling reading comprehension in all subject areas?

7 Writing Strategies for ELs and Struggling Writers

ELs are not simply learning English; they are using their second language to access the curriculum in content areas such as science, social studies, language arts, and mathematics. One of the challenges they face in schools relates to the literacy demands of these content area courses. Specifically, ELs must produce writing that not only proves their knowledge of challenging academic content but also meets teachers' expectations for the "genres" of writing appropriate to their subject areas.

> Nationally, students today are not meeting the basic writing standards (National Commission on Writing, 2005).

TEACHING ELS TO READ AND WRITE

ELs come to school to learn the academic English they need to understand, discuss, read, and write in the content area. They do double the work in the mainstream classrooms (Short & Fitzsimmons, 2007). Thus content teachers become reading and writing teachers by doing the following:

- ✓ Emphasizing the reading and writing practices specific to their subject
- ✓ Bridging ELs' reading comprehension levels, building background, and strengthening English proficiency (Calderón, 2007; Carnegie Council on Advancing Adolescent Literacy, 2010).

Proficient readers are not always proficient writers. Although reading and writing skills complement each other, they do not always go hand in hand. Many adolescents are able to handle reading demands but may encounter difficulties with writing. A brief comparison is presented in Table 7.1.

Table 7.1 Similarities and Differences Between Reading and Writing	
Similarities	Differences
• Reading and writing draw from the same pool of background knowledge, for example, a general understanding of the attributes of texts.	• Readers form a mental representation of thoughts written by someone else. • Writers formulate their own thoughts, organize them, and create a written record of them using the conventions of spelling and grammar.
• Reading and writing are vital aspects of literacy.	• Reading and writing require their own dedicated instruction. • What improves reading does not always improve writing and vice versa.

Source: Graham and Perin, 2007

Also, students need to become flexible writers in the classroom and outside the classroom—such as in the workplace, the home, the community, and so forth. In order for ELs to develop the adequate writing skills to meet high school classroom demands, they need to do the following:

✓ Develop academic English through the four language domains
✓ Become proficient in the content area knowledge
✓ Wrestle with the details and facts of texts
✓ Produce original products incorporating language and concepts to communicate with others

Literacy encompasses both reading and writing skills. If students are to learn, they must write. Lack of writing proficiency has been recognized as an intrinsic part of this national literacy crisis.

> College instructors estimate that 50% of high school graduates are not prepared for college-level writing (Achieve, Inc., 2005).

Effective content-area writing pedagogy for ELs includes communicative competence in a range of written genres that provide meaningful, authentic writing experiences in the content areas. Building on students' existing expertise, developing student autonomy, making genre expectations explicit, and encouraging peer collaboration are all promising practices.

Genres

Genres are different forms of writing, such as poems, plays, or novels. Specific categories include adventure novels, romance novels, and so forth. In a broader sense, genres may also encompass various communication events like a TV show, a newspaper report, a wedding ceremony, a joke, or a court trial script. Each genre has specific characteristics that make it different from other genres, such as specific purpose, overall structure, and linguistic—grammar and word usage—features (Gibbons, 2002).

Writing to learn means that students adapt their writing to the context in which it takes place. Writing in the content classroom plays two complementary but distinct roles:

- First, writing draws on the use of strategies, for example, planning, evaluating, and revising text, to accomplish a variety of tasks—such as writing a report or expressing an opinion with the support of evidence.
- Second, writing is a means of extending and deepening students' knowledge. It is a tool for learning subject matter.

Because these two roles are closely linked, content area teachers need to provide instruction and practice in reading and writing in their specific discipline. Table 7.2 illustrates the genres or types of writing for specific subject areas.

Table 7.2 Genres or Types of Writing for Content Areas			
Math	*Science*	*Social Studies*	*Language Arts*
• Graphs • Problems • Proposals • Journals • Procedures/ explanations • Proofs • Tables • Notes/ observations	• Lab reports • Field notes • Explanations • Arguments • Research papers • Persuasive essays • Written debates • Journals • Science fiction novels or short stories	• Factual/narrative descriptions • Persuasive essays • Compare and contrast essays • Arguments • Written debates • Discussions of authors' intentions and perspectives • Biographies	• Narratives • Biographies • Travelogues • Plays • Letters • Interviews • Newspaper articles • Poetry

Source: Scarcella, 2005

The report commissioned by the Carnegie Corporation of New York, *Writing Next*, identifies 11 elements of effective adolescent writing instruction (Graham & Perin, 2007). We have added notes on their relevancy, possibilities, or effectiveness for ELs after each description:

1. Writing Strategies. This involves explicitly and systematically teaching students the steps necessary for planning, revising, and/or editing their compositions. The goal is to teach students to use these steps independently. Strategy instruction for ELs includes them as active collaborators in the learning process as they do the following:

> > Develop background knowledge
>
>   o Become aware of the purpose and benefits of the strategy.
>   o Practice it after the teacher models how to use the strategy.
>   o Memorize the steps of the strategy and any accompanying mnemonic devices.
>   o Use the supports or scaffolds provided by the teacher for mastery of the strategy.
>   o Use the strategy independently with few or no supports.

The Writing Strategy for ELs. This strategy can be used to meet the needs of ELs. You scaffold all the elements from building background to providing words and text models for the writing. ELs will need continuous support throughout the writing. Ask students to use as many new (academic) words from the chapter as possible, and count how many they have actually used. Beginning ELs may benefit from writing shorter sentences from the grade-level text and will need noun-verb-object combinations, adjectives before nouns, adverbs, and punctuation. Their writing can consist of three or four sentences. Later on, after several accurate attempts, they will need prompts for compound sentences, clauses, and style in order to write four or five sentences for accuracy at first and then proceed to larger accurate writing output.

2. Summarization. This involves explicitly and systematically teaching students how to summarize texts.

The Summarization Strategy for ELs. Summarization is an effective language function and reading comprehension skill that needs to be used in writing. When ELs have been explicitly taught sentence starters for summarization, they can transfer these into their writing. Summaries help students review and remember information. ELs *explain* what they have learned through a summary and write a report about what they have learned. Useful sentence starters include the following:

    o The author is telling us that . . .
    o The author is comparing . . . with . . .
    o We read about . . . and discovered
    o For me, this means that . . .

3. Collaborative/Cooperative Writing. This involves instructional arrangements for students to work together and plan, draft, revise, and edit their compositions.

Collaborative/Cooperative Writing for ELs. Collaborative or cooperative writing is a useful tool for ELs. They plan, draft, write, and edit in pairs or teams of four and enrich language and ideas. There are also cooperative learning activities, discussed in Chapter 8, such as **Write-Around,** where, after reading, the math teacher assigns a sentence starter such as the following:

When the Sunshine School sixth graders tried to light a bulb, they decided to _____

_____

_____

The experiment was _____

_____

_____

So next time they need to _____

_____

_____

Remind students to use as many vocabulary words as possible from their word wall or vocabulary list. Students are sitting in teams of four and each completes the sentence starter. Next, they pass their paper to the right and read the paper they received from the student on their left. They read the sentence and add a sentence that goes along with that one. Thus, they continue to write, read, and pass the paper for about 10 minutes. Once they have sufficient writing, the teacher asks them to do a **Read-Around,** where students read the story/summary that they are holding when the time is called. The team selects the one they like best for revising, editing, and reading to the class. They add a title, a powerful conclusion, quotes, and so forth, to enrich the selected piece. Since spelling and grammar corrections are to be made afterward, the ELs feel comfortable about writing because they know the team will help correct or interpret afterward.

4. Setting Specific Product Goals. This involves assigning students specific reachable goals for the writing they are to complete. It includes identifying the purpose of the assignment, for example, to persuade, and also characteristics of the final product.

Product Goals for ELs. Beginning ELs need prompts and samples for regular letter writing and for persuasive letter writing. Advanced ELs will need prompts, samples, and extensive practice for argumentative discourse, including a statement of belief, two or three reasons for that belief, reasons why others might disagree, and why those reasons are incorrect.

Writing Frames is a strategy to summarize content area information that adheres to a basic structure (Color in Colorado, 2010). Beginning ELs follow the organizational pattern to summarize content information using partially completed sentences and transition words and phrases. Students would benefit from the following frames or versions of them adapted to grade and content levels.

Sample Compare-Contrast Frame. This frame can be used in content areas with expository texts. Students write similarities and differences between facts, ideas, events, people, places, and processes.

_____ are different from _____ in several ways. First, _____
_____, while
_____.
Additionally, _____
_____, whereas
_____
_____. They are alike in that _____
and _____.
So, it is evident that_____
_____.

First, model how to use the writing frame. Make your students feel comfortable. If needed, scaffold one writing frame at a time and allow time for students to write their responses. If you use a modified version of the text, keep the same essential grade-level content while attending to the language proficiency needs.

Sample Chronological Order Frame. The chronological order frame is best used with information that is temporally sequenced, such as information from a history text.

At the end of _____, what happened was that
_____.
Prior to this, _____.
Before that, however, _____
_____. This whole sequence of events
began when _____.
The most important event to occur was _____
because _____.

Sample Narrative Plot Frame. The narrative frame helps students summarize core plot elements from a story.

In this story, the problem starts when _____
_____.
Then, _____.
Next, _____.
Finally, the problem is solved when _____
_____.
In the end, _____
_____.
The lesson I learned from reading this story was _____
_____.

5. Word Processing. Computer and word-processing devices are particularly useful to low achieving writers. Students may work collaboratively on writing assignments using personal laptop computers. Also, they may learn to word-process a composition under teacher guidance. Typing text on the computer with word-processing software produces a neat and legible script. It allows the writer to add, delete, and move text easily. Word-processing software includes spell checkers.

Word Processing for ELs. Typing text on the computer with word-processing software will help ELs see their writing in a neat format where it is easy to add, delete, use spell-check, look up words in the dictionary or a bilingual dictionary, and/or add pictures where they lack words. Computers also facilitate cooperative writing. ELs like to create PowerPoint slides because they can write quick quips.

6. Sentence Combining. This involves teaching students to construct more complex and sophisticated sentences through exercises in which two or more basic sentences are combined into a single sentence. It is an alternative approach to more traditional grammar instruction.

Sentence Combining for ELs. Beginning ELs use the context of what they are reading and use connectors such as ***and, but, so***, and ***because***. As they become more advanced, they will have the concept of "sentence combining" as they practice embedding different types of clauses and phrases into compound complex sentences.

7. Prewriting. Students engage in activities designed to help them generate or organize ideas for their composition. Activities include the following: (a) gathering information for a paper through reading or developing a visual representation of their ideas before sitting down to write, (b) encouraging group and individual planning before writing, (c) organizing prewriting activities, (d) prompting students to plan after providing a brief demonstration of how to do so, and (e) assigning reading material pertinent to a topic and then encouraging students to plan their work in advance.

Prewriting for ELs. ELs need guidance, extra time, examples, and prompts to use graphic organizers and they need brainstorming to be able to pull their thoughts together into sentences. Graphic organizers can be introduced for summarization of ideas at first. Then, when students have grasped a couple of examples, other organizers can be introduced for prewriting and later on to retell a story or report that they have written.

8. Inquiry Activities. Students engage in activities that help them develop ideas and content for a particular writing task by analyzing immediate concrete data—such as comparing and contrasting cases or collecting and evaluating evidence. Characteristics include the following: (a) a clearly specified goal (e.g., describe this situation), (b) an analysis of concrete and immediate data (e.g., observe peers during a specific activity), (c) use of specific strategies to conduct analysis (e.g., ask peers to observe the reason for a particular action), and (d) application of what was learned (e.g., assign the writing of a story incorporating insights from the inquiry process).

Inquiry Activities for ELs. Beginning ELs can use charts, lists of content words, and those academic words that nest the content and graphic organizers as prewriting and writing activities.

The **Jigsaw Content Learning** or **Expert Jigsaw** strategy can be used as a means of learning from multiple source materials on a topic.

Expert Jigsaw

- o Students form Expert teams (all the No. 1s together, No. 2s, No. 3s, No. 4s).
- o Each team is responsible for one part of a topic source material (e.g., website passage, audio-taped lecture, magazine article, story, problem, newspaper report, video, brochure, textbook chapter).
- o Each team studies, discusses, and summarizes the content using a writing frame, illustrated in No. 4 in this chapter.
- o Each team prepares one or two test questions.
- o Each Expert goes back to the home team and teaches the others. Expert groups use their frames to summarize the material (each member will need a copy of the frame).
- o Students return to home groups to share, in turn, each member's summary from their respective source material.
- o Each Expert gives the test to the team.
- o The questions are used for the real test.

Modifications can include summarizing the content using a graphic organizer, a double-entry journal, and so forth.

9. Process Writing Approach. Students work in a workshop environment and benefit from extended opportunities for writing. See the following for examples: (a) emphasizing writing for real audiences; (b) encouraging cycles of planning, translating, and reviewing; (c) stressing personal responsibility and ownership of writing projects; (d) facilitating high levels of student interactions; (e) developing supportive writing environments; (f) encouraging self-reflection and evaluation; and (g) offering personalized individual assistance, brief instructional lessons to meet students' individual needs, and also more extended and systematic instruction.

The Process Writing Approach for ELs. ELs benefit when process writing or writing workshops are collaborative with cooperative learning and sentence combining activities and when they read good models of texts that contain the elements teachers want to see in their writing.

10. Study of Models. Students have plenty of opportunities to read, analyze, and emulate models of good writing. They analyze these examples and emulate the critical elements, patterns, and forms embodied in the models in their own writing.

Model for ELs. ELs benefit greatly from models of quality writing. Provide them with one brief, well-written, simple piece each week so that students can emulate it. Have them gradually experiment with each genre (e.g., letters, stories, poems, point of view writing, expository genres). Ask students to highlight the connectors, sentence starters, punctuation, and other features, then to apply some of the same features to their writing.

11. Writing for Content Learning. Students use writing as a tool for learning content material. Writing-to-learn activities are equally effective for all content areas.

Writing for Content Learning for ELs. ELs need extensive content writing or writing for content mastery (e.g., main point and supporting evidence writing, biographies, lab reports, inquiry research reports, essays, persuasive writing). Expository writing patterns include presenting a main point and supporting it with concrete evidence. Students are able to do the following: (a) analyze and explain; (b) show relationships between idea and concepts, such as explaining democracy or photosynthesis or provide examples of an author's craft, such as foreshadowing, and steps for solving a problem; (c) make a claim or take a position while supporting it with details and evidence; and, (d) use a logical organization with complex sentence structures (compound sentences, embedded clauses) and connectors (supports, reflects, symbols).

Some Strategies for Collaborative Writing, Revising, and Editing

There are fun and effective cooperative learning strategies for drafting, writing, revising, and editing. Chapter 8 includes a number of cooperative learning and classroom management strategies that might be helpful in developing the four language skills. They can be conducted in teams or with pairs of students.

Revision Through *Cut and Grow*

Jeanne Cantu from San Antonio, Texas, uses the *Cut and Grow* activity after a *Write-Around* activity or individual writing for revising and editing. This revision technique helps students layer and bring depth to their writing.

Students need the following supplies:

- Their compositions
- A blank sheet of paper, preferably another color
- Scissors
- Tape

Procedure for Students:

1. Find a sentence in the composition that lacks specificity and detail.

2. Do not choose the first or last sentences in a paragraph.

3. Add information to the sentence that will enhance or give depth to the idea.

4. Use more Tier 2 and Tier 3 words.

Here's an example of an original sentence from a first draft composition:

> The price of gas is high.

Here is the elaborated sentence/idea:

> Gas is so expensive that I can only afford to put in $15 at a time. I used to let my brother borrow my car and wouldn't worry about the gas. Now, I make him pay me every time he uses it.

5. Have students write their elaborated sentences on the colored sheet of paper.

6. Have students cut their compositions right below their unelaborated sentence and tape it onto the colored sheet. Then, have them tape the rest of the composition to the colored sheet.

7. Students can immediately see how their paper has "grown" and been improved through this revision strategy.

Another Editing Strategy, Often Called Ratiocination

1. Students create a chart with three columns.

2. Students label the columns as follows: Code, Clue, Decoding.

3. The teacher directs the students to check their papers for a particular purpose, such as overuse of the "to be" verbs.

4. Teachers may need to do a minilesson before the particular skill is checked for and edited.

5. Teachers should start by checking for one clue per paper and add more as the students learn the process.

6. Students should have colored markers, pencils, or crayons available for this activity.

Table 7.3 Chart for Ratiocination		
Code – Make a list of every first word	*Clue*	*Decoding*
Circle	"to be" verbs: is, am, are, was, were, be, being, been	• do not change • change to a vivid verb • indicate passive voice • indicate a weak sentence • do not change if the "to be" verb is in a quote or dialogue
Rectangle They	first word in every sentence	• do not change • vary sentence beginnings

Assessing Writing

Writing has to be intensive for ELs throughout the secondary school years. The development and progress of their narrative, informative, explanatory, persuasive, argument styles should be monitored. Exit Passes and different types of writing can be collected in portfolios for comparing writing progress month by month. Rubrics and criteria like the following can be used for scaffolding and monitoring writing progress.

A four-step rubric can be used for EL writing samples:

Level 1—novice

Level 2—intermediate

Level 3—competent

Level 4—exceptional

Each level can be defined according to the criteria of the assignment and grade level. Some students may be a Level 4 in their native language and need only concentrate on learning new English words, transition words, idioms, and cultural referents. Other students may be a Level 1 in their own language. These students will need a lot of work with all aspects of literacy. They will need considerably more time and more direct teaching to catch up with all others.

Table 7.4 · Criteria/Rubrics

Conventions	Punctuation	Capitalization	Word Usage	Grammar/Syntax	Writer's Craft
Legible writing/ No typos	Period at the end of each telling sentence	Capitalize proper nouns (names of people, pets, places, institutions, etc.)	Words used seem right when read aloud	Use the correct verb form with each noun	Use brainstorming or graphic organizer to plan
Sentences are complete	Question mark at the end of each question	Capitalize the pronoun I	Use synonyms instead of repeating words	Use correct word order in sentences (adjective, noun)	Describe setting
Sentences begin in different ways	Exclamation mark at the end of exclamatory sentences	Capitalize the first word in a sentence	Use words that are precise/specific	Use pronouns that agree with gender	Describe what characters look like
Legible writing/ No typos	Period at the end of each telling sentence	Capitalize proper nouns (names of people, pets, places, institutions, etc.)	Words used seem right when read aloud	Use the correct verb form with each noun	Select purpose: Explain or inform; persuade or argue a point/opinion
Sentences are complete	Question mark at the end of each question	Capitalize the pronoun	Use synonyms instead of repeating words	Use correct word order in sentences (adjective, noun)	Select organizational structure, format: • Description • Sequence, chronological order • Cause, effect • Compare, contrast • Problem, solution
Sentences begin in different ways	Exclamation mark at the end of exclamatory sentences	Capitalize first word in a sentence	Use words that are precise/specific	Use pronouns that agree with gender	Use a topic sentence to introduce the topic clearly

Differentiated Growth Plan

Where does an EL start in the writing process in an all-English class? The ELs should tackle the same writing assignments as all other students but on a much smaller scale at the beginning. A rule of thumb might be to let the student write only one paragraph and use only three or four of the new vocabulary words and some invented spelling and creative grammatical structures around the first three weeks of school. This will give the teacher time to analyze the students' writing and work out a plan of action with the student. The student can work on one or two skills per week. The proofreading and editing will focus on these skills. Increasingly, the student and teacher will target other skills that can be assessed in the context of the class assignment. These contracts and samples of skill mastery can be included in the student's portfolio. After a few months, the student's growth will be quite evident from the contents in the portfolio.

The Time Element

Time definitely will be a factor in mastery of language and content. ELs cannot be expected to finish as many exercises as does a fluent English speaker. Exercises have to be carefully selected and trimmed down to a few good examples that reflect progress of skills and content on which the student.

ELs handle twice as many variables and perform twice as many cognitive tasks in any one class as their peers. Therefore, help ELs feel free to experiment with language while they are learning content. Your role is to make sure that there are ample opportunities for them to practice the use of these new "norms of expression" through individual, pair, and cooperative activities.

Questions and Topics for Discussion

1. What are the writing needs of your ELs and other students? Is it academic vocabulary, grammar, editing, revising, or something else?

2. How many students need tutoring? How many are beginning ELs?

3. How many are learning to write? How many are writing to learn?

4. What will your differentiated growth plan to adapt and incorporate selected writing strategies in your content classroom look like?

5. Which strategies are more appropriate for ELs' grade and language proficiency levels? Which strategies are more appropriate for struggling writers?

8

Engaging ELs via Cooperative Learning and Classroom Management

Adolescent students pose a number of challenges. These challenges range from legal and economic issues in their communities to academic issues stemming from a history of poor achievement. One of the challenges is how to engage those students who seem reluctant or disengaged in the classroom. They appear to be unmotivated and demonstrate a careless attitude about learning and succeeding at school.

LT-ELs in secondary schools have great difficulty fitting in because of academic or language status. Sometimes, they are labeled and excluded from participation in learning tasks. If these students do not pass state exams, they face serious consequences, including not being promoted to the next grade or not graduating. Although most ELs enter school eager to learn, it is not surprising that many eventually become discouraged, lose their motivation, and become reluctant or disengaged.

Challenges in My Classroom

Some students perform poorly on tests and earn low grades.

They experience difficulties at home.

They have problems with peers during class breaks and in the classroom.

They experience mood changes.

One argues with me loudly . . .

Schools need to find the means to educate reluctant students, to address their needs and reach out to them. Fortunately, there are strategies that can help us meet these challenges by motivating students to participate under low anxiety conditions. The school's responsibility to consistently acquire new knowledge about instruction in order to do better by students and lead educators' roles to engage all students in learning include the following:

- A positive school climate that sparks enthusiasm and boosts confidence
- School leader/student and teacher/student direct communication with plenty of opportunities for positive relations in the students' academic life that promote a love for school
- A challenging, rigorous, but involving and motivating classroom environment
- Exciting strategies and age-related techniques to engage students in learning tasks

What Does Not Help?

- Dealing with reluctant school systems, schools, administrators, and teachers
- Blaming low achievement and lack of class participation on the ELs and/or reluctant students and their families
- Having low expectations through tracking and low level classes
- Making it difficult to reach students by teaching in the same ineffective teacher-centered ways

The United States is at a tipping point to enable ELs and all students to succeed in a global economy—one where the students and teachers cocreate and coconstruct meaning and coherence from a wide array of individual experiences and ways of learning. For example, there is wide consensus that today's students need creativity and other "21st-century skills" in order to interact in a new age of technological advances, environmental awareness, and globalization (Pink, 2005; Rotherham & Willingham, 2009).

Teacher quality continues to be one of the most important factors affecting student engagement and achievement. Effective professional development needs to improve the school experiences of disengaged students and include strategies for teaching, motivating students, and making their work comprehensible in the classroom. Effective teachers use cooperative learning and/or classroom management strategies to promote and encourage the participation of every student in their classrooms. By the same token, teachers also need to build a school culture and sensitization that foster behaviors and attitudes that contribute positively to teaching and reaching students.

> A motivating environment, a trust fund, cultivates intellectual development, college preparation, and career development.

USING COOPERATIVE LEARNING TO HELP ENGAGE ELS AND ALL STUDENTS

Cooperative learning is a successful teaching and motivating strategy. Small teams composed of students with different levels of ability use a variety of learning activities to improve their understanding of a subject under low anxiety conditions (Calderón et al., 1998).

ELs at all levels of language proficiency can benefit from cooperative learning.

Beginning ELs can also use their first language as they build the academic and linguistic skills they need to make progress in the content area (Calderón, 1994; McGroarty & Calderón, 2005).

These cooperative learning norms and protocols help us teach and reach students in the content and language classrooms. A poster can be a reminder to students of what is expected at each activity. Our goal is quality instruction, and incorporating these tools in our lessons can provide us with the means for students to succeed. Furthermore, our focus should be on tasks, not roles.

> Each team member is responsible for learning what is taught and for helping teammates learn, thus creating an atmosphere of achievement.
> (Johnson & Johnson, 1987, p. 73)

Table 8.1	Social Norms and Protocols in Cooperative Learning
Norms	*Protocols*
Everyone contributes ideas.	• Respect others. Be positive. • Accept opinions.
Everyone has a specific task (not role).	• Contribute to the discussions.
Everyone learns from one another.	• Help others. • Accept help.
Everyone works with an open mind.	• Stay on task. • Accept responsibility.

> When students are given specific **tasks**, they are responsible for their own performance during the cooperative learning activity. The final product is the sum of individual performances on activities to accomplish the concerted project (Calderón, 2001).

> Why *not* assign **roles?** Role assignment is not productive in instruction as students are expected to perform in only one way in the activity. For example, "In this team, you are the writer . . . You are the discussant . . . You are the time keeper . . . You are the presenter . . . etc." By dissecting the cooperative learning activity and assigning these roles, we limit the equal exposure, opportunity, and access to rigorous content all students need to have as well as exposure to reading, writing, discussing, and analyzing in order to develop such skills. See the following, for example:

  o The time keeper will only remind her peers how many minutes are left to complete the activity. She will not be directly involved with the academic work.
  o The writer will have little or no opportunity to get involved in discussing, debating, or sharing his opinions as he will have to focus on note taking only.
  o And so on.

CONDITIONS FOR PRODUCTIVE COOPERATIVE LEARNING

We learn something when we have the opportunity to discuss it with a peer or peers. Cooperative learning is a needed resource in content area classrooms with ELs across all English acquisition levels. For example, cooperative learning strategies can be used to engage ELs in motivating content area settings while meeting important learning goals. Your role is to monitor, prompt, and praise students and address their concerns.

My Cooperative Learning Plan

What do I want my students to learn from the task?

How do I assess them? How do I group them? How do I time the activity?

Choose a cooperative learning activity that best fits your lesson and incorporate it in your plan. Before you begin the activity, remind your students of the social norms and protocols posted in the classroom. Remind them of what is expected of them: You have assigned them specific tasks; each is responsible for his or her own performance and each team member needs to contribute equally to the final product.

Social Rules

- There is no "hitchhiking" or "freeloading" for anyone on a team.

- Individual accountability: Team members feel in charge of their own and their teammates' learning.

- Team members have the opportunity to learn and to express learning in ways that facilitate their success.

The conditions for productive cooperative efforts include the following:

- *Positive Interdependence* or *"We are in this together,"* when each team member's efforts is required and indispensable for team success, and each member contributes to the joint effort.
- *Face-to-Face Interaction* to explain orally, teach one another, and check for understanding.
- *Individual and Group Accountability* to prevent students from social loafing; each student makes an active contribution to the team.
- *Interpersonal and Small-Group Skills* for students to develop social skills for leadership, decision making, and trust building.
- *Group Processing* for reflection on how well they are working together and how they might do better as a learning team (Johnson & Johnson, 1987, 1992).

These conditions lead us to involve all students, while attending to their specific needs, through pacing and complexity.

COOPERATIVE LEARNING AND CLASSROOM MANAGEMENT

As with cooperative learning, classroom management strategies support teaching and learning. As classroom managers, we set rules and procedures for students to be orderly and respectful. We try to win students over, not win over them. At most public schools, effective classroom management has been recognized as a crucial element in effective teaching.

In cooperative learning groups, students are more academically productive, better behaved, and less likely to drop out (Center for Public Education, 2008). A caring classroom environment with high academic expectations is more effective in producing learning. Classroom management, effective instructional strategies, and pacing and complexity of content area are three components that complement each other in teaching and learning. Students may have difficulty learning if there are no management rules set for the academic task or when the instructional strategies are not strategically differentiated to their specific individual needs.

What Students Want From Their Teachers

Take me seriously.

Challenge me to think.

Tell me I can do it.

Show me how.

Tap my creativity.

Bring out my best self.

In a well-managed classroom, teaching and learning can flourish, and the teacher is most responsible for creating this atmosphere for students of all achievement levels regardless of the levels of heterogeneity in the class. Here are some helpful tips:

> Recognize or reward successful teams.
> Ensure that students are responsible for their own performance and that they develop content mastery, efficacy, and ownership in learning.
> Set up a scoring system for students of all performance levels to contribute meaningfully to the team scores or products.

Your reward system should reward students for improving their level of performance over their usual level. In this way, all students are motivated to do their best. Your system rewards improvement in performance rather than ability so that students can succeed based on their own efforts.

Team members in the benchmark category—those students who present the least challenges in the classroom—tutor their peers who need the support to either the strategic and/or the intensive group. These two groups of students might be otherwise ignored in the classroom or unwilling to learn because they would be perceived as unlikely to contribute much to the team score. This does not happen when an effective teacher structures activities that balance the challenge and support necessary to enhance the students' willingness to risk the hard work of real learning (Tomlinson, 2008).

USING COOPERATIVE LEARNING IN CONTENT CLASSES

You can achieve 100% student participation in the learning task, in all lessons and contents, with all students, including ELs, at all levels of language proficiency. You can incorporate cooperative learning strategies in math, science, social studies, and language arts classrooms and engage all students on vocabulary, reading and writing development as part of a lesson, chapter, or unit.

By using cooperative learning strategies in my content classroom, I can do the following:

- Consolidate or anchor knowledge of the content lesson, so that all or most of my students know the content and use the correct terms, along with proper grammar.
- Check whether everyone understood the content, what they know, what still is missing, and what I need to make this work in future classes.
- Assess and address the unique needs of my students, including those who are ELs and those who are reluctant to participate.

Cooperative learning permeates all lessons by building on students' cooperation and engagement and on classroom management so that class time is not wasted. Students follow the set norms and protocols and are on task in a quality learning environment.

The following selection of cooperative learning strategies can assist you in strengthening your instruction of the academic content in English for ELs and their peers. As you facilitate these strategies, you continue to be an effective teacher because you provide for interaction through heterogeneous groupings. Also, you continue to motivate ELs to use English with a peer or peers in a safe context.

A MYRIAD OF COOPERATIVE LEARNING STRATEGIES

The following strategies (see box) are research-based and have been proven successful in meeting the linguistic and academic needs of ELs across all levels of language proficiency (Calderón, 2007). You can choose the ones that best meet the chapter or unit's instructional objectives. These strategies can be aligned with grade-level curriculum and content area standards and built on the foundation of effective classroom management. By using them in your lessons, you can balance nurturing with setting clear limits and high standards of responsibility in all your students. You also encourage them to be independent while guiding them without controlling. These are the strategies that have been proven instrumental in quality teaching and reaching students.

Characteristics of _____

1. Three-Step Interview

2. Group Investigation

3. Random Numbers

4. In-House Jigsaw

5. Expert Jigsaw

6. Partners

7. Line Ups

8. Tear Ups

9. Corners

10. Tea Party

11. Exit Pass

The 11 cooperative learning strategies included here do not exclude the use of additional ones you may have in your repertoire. Careful planning and deciding on the cooperative learning strategy ahead of time assure the greater effectiveness with student learning in a well-managed classroom.

My suggested plan can include the following:

- The cooperative learning strategy
- The learning goals (grade-level contents and academic language)
- Instructions on how to anchor knowledge and assess their level of understanding (individual, group)
- Knowledge and language skills to be taught (vocabulary, reading, writing, grammar)
- Instructions on how to group students (four to six students, heterogeneous)
- Necessary materials
- Time assigned for the tasks

Let's not assume that students already know how to work in groups and proceed to model to them how to work together. Teamwork is increasingly valued in the workplace today; all students can learn these valuable skills. Be explicit about the value of cooperative learning; students need to know what benefits to expect from participating in this instructional strategy. By grouping them, all group members work through the assignment, understand it, and complete it. They strive for mutual benefit so that all team members gain from each other's efforts (Johnson & Johnson, 1987).

Characteristics of My Teaching

- Fold paper into eight rectangles.
- Write eight characteristics about _____ (the content).
- Mill around and find a partner with matching characteristics (no talking).
- Walk together and find two partners who are different.
- Sit together as a team.

This activity and the next activity, Three-Step Interview, can be used at the beginning of the school year to form heterogeneous groupings. They also can be used during the year for reseating purposes to start a new activity. Activity 1 can be conducted with a different topic (e.g., college interests, science projects, experiences visiting a museum, hobbies, favorite movies, life goals).

Three-Step Interview

Step 1—Students are in pairs; one is the interviewer and the other the interviewee (1 minute).

Step 2—Students reverse roles (1 minute).

Step 3—Students number off (Nos. 1–4) and take turns sharing with the team what they learned about their partner in the interview (1 minute each—don't stop before the minute is up; finish your sentence when the time is called).

Facilitate the Interview With a Positive Essence Perspective

✓ Wonderful ones, share what you have learned from terrific twos with your team.

✓ Thrilling threes, share what you have learned from fantastic fours with your team.

And so on . . .

Remind the interviewers to follow the interviewee's chosen topic and that the purpose of the interview is to gather information to share with teammates. Instruct students and model to look for themes in the interview responses that will help them capture the positive essence of the peer. Also, as you use both activities in ensuing lessons, you can change the topics to match the specific goals of the content area.

Group Investigation

- Students propose topics and categorize suggestions.
- They organize into research groups to plan the learning task or subtopics for investigation.
- Individual students gather and evaluate data and synthesize findings into a group report.
- Each research group presents to the entire class and actively involves the audience.
- Teachers and students evaluate student learning.

Group representatives form a steering committee to coordinate plans for the final report presentation. You evaluate students' higher level thinking about the subject they studied and how they did the following:

- Investigated aspects of the subject
- Applied their knowledge to the solutions of new problems

- Used inferences from what they learned in discussing questions requiring analysis and judgment
- Reached conclusions from sets of data

In order to make Group Investigation work best in your classroom, you may want to focus on and support interpersonal dialogue. You may also want to consider the affective-social dimension of learning. Your role during this activity is as a resource person and facilitator. But you also need to model the social and communication skills expected from your students.

Random Numbers

- Write your first name on a 3 x 5 card and also write three random numbers between 1 and 20.
- Share with your teams and give a reason for the numbers you chose.

This activity can be used at the beginning of the class to build background knowledge and review concepts from previous classes. See the following, for example:

2, 3, 5. I am reading 2 short stories. Then I have to write a review with 3 paragraphs for each. Both reviews are due in 5 days.

12, 4, 16. I used 12 of the 16 new words and 4 of them were cognates.

Use Random Numbers as a warm-up, a "do-now," or a bell ringer. Change the sequence and numbers occasionally. Students can share with a peer, their team, or you can call to the whole class in popcorn style.

In-House Jigsaw

- Each student is responsible for one part of a chapter, story, or problem.
- Each provides the others in the team with the information.
- Each prepares one or two test questions.

You can incorporate jigsaws with any content that can be divided into sections. Your learning goals include content concepts rather than skills.

This jigsaw is a simple in-team activity; you identify a passage, a text, or a problem and divide it into equal parts. Each team member becomes an expert on that part and prepares two questions, presents her piece, and tests peers at the end of the presentation. Each member reads, summarizes, and prepares to teach the team. Suggested activities include reading the following and using higher order thinking skill questions:

A story

A chapter

A social studies narrative

A biography

Descriptive science or math materials

Expert Jigsaw

- Students form Expert teams (First, they number up at their tables, 1, 2, etc. Then, all the No. 1s go together, then No. 2s, then No. 3s, then No. 4s.).
- Each team is responsible for one part of a chapter, story, or problem.
- Each team studies, discusses, and summarizes the content.
- Each prepares one or two test questions.
- Each Expert goes back to the home team and teaches the others.
- Each Expert gives the test to the team.
- The questions are used for the real test.

The Expert Jigsaw is conducted by Expert teams outside the group, as follows:

1. Task division: A task, passage, text, or problem is divided into equal parts.

2. Home groups: Each team member is given a topic on which to become an Expert.

3. Expert groups: Students who have the same topics meet to discuss the topics, master them, and plan how to teach them.

4. Home groups: Students return to their original groups and teach what they learned to their team members.

5. All students take the same test individually.

By using the Expert Jigsaw in class, students become motivated to study the material well and to work hard in their Expert groups so that they can help their team do well. The key to Jigsaw is interdependence. Remind them that students depend on their teammates to provide the information needed to succeed on the assessments.

Partners

- Students work in pairs to create or master content.
- They consult with partners from other teams.
- They then present their products or understanding of contents with the other partner pair in their team.

Explain to your students that this activity is very important for them. In Partners they are motivated to do academic work and feel that their classmates want them to do their best. They exert social pressure on one another to achieve. In this way, they maintain behavior that helps them succeed. Continue to facilitate as with the other activities. Focus on quality interaction among students that enhances learning tasks. This interaction is what leads to improved student achievement. Students learn from one another because, in their discussions of the content, cognitive conflicts will arise, inadequate reasoning will be exposed, and higher quality understanding will emerge.

Line Ups!

- Mill around and Line Up according to the task or question.
- Count off 1 to 4, or as indicated, and form a team.
- Sit together as a team.

Tear Ups!

- Each team tears two sheets of different-colored construction paper into creative pieces.
- Share your piece with your team and talk about it. What does it look like?
- Write a group story with plot, characters, and background setting.
- Paste the pieces beside the story of that match.
- Share your story.

Tear Ups! requires more time to accomplish than Line Ups! Both activities can focus on writing projects. See the following, for example:

- Students are to engage in a comprehensive writing project where they work together as a team to plan, draft, revise, and edit their story.
- Team writing can be simple compositions prepared as oral recitations to be presented as poems, raps, or choral readings.
- Individual writing can be simple summaries on Exit Passes or learning logs of what students learned that day, week, and so forth.

The writing activity helps ELs and reluctant students. They take part in mapping a story line, drawing a protagonist's personality, and adding visuals or drawings to the story. These visuals help them see the relationships they need to verbalize. You can also facilitate and continue to motivate when certain processes are just too difficult for them to write about. These are supporting activities to engage reluctant students and facilitate their academic writing:

- Illustrations
- Guiding questions of prompts
- Sample grammar structures
- Immediate teacher feedback of work submitted
- More opportunities and guidance for student self-review and editing of student's work

Corners

- Count from 1 to 9 (No. 1s go to one corner, No. 2s to another, and so forth, to form triads).
- Timed Team Share (30 seconds each): First student answers question, next student adds to the answer, next student does the same, process continues. (90 seconds)

Corners allows for regrouping into triads at the end of a lesson. It is a quick activity that gets students out of their seats and gives them the opportunity to interact with other students since the triads are randomly selected. Pose selected questions to students with a set time so that they concentrate on the responses. You say "30" to indicate that it is time for the next person to answer or to add to what has already been said. Use an alternative last question like the following: *Come up with a cheer or a chant to reflect the group's effort or the fact that you are happy to work with this team.* Or you can say the following: *Write your answers with different colors on a poster or chart.*

Tea Party

- Count off No. 1 and No. 2.
- No. 1s form an inside circle.
- No. 2s form the outside circle.
- Make sure you have a partner facing you (shake hands).
- You have 1 minute to discuss a question.
- When the minute is up, say good-bye, move to the right, find a new partner, shake hands, and get ready to discuss the next question.

Prepare a list of questions related to the lesson just completed. Make the Tea Party a reward activity for student accomplishments. Celebrate their effort once a month or every two months by bringing their preferred music and play it after they say "good-bye" to the partner and before they say "hello" to the new peer; they dance their way to meet the next peer. Concentric circles can also be replaced by conga lines, with the variation that the student at the head of the line dances her way to the end of the line if she so chooses, while the peers clap to the tune.

Tea Party weekly variations:

1. The inner circle is given the definition of the words while the outer circle is given the vocabulary words. Both groups work on the answer.

2. When there is insufficient space, two or three concentric circles are formed in different areas of the class.

Exit Pass

- Teams or individual students write one thing they learned today and one question they have on a sticky note or piece of paper. Make sure they write their name and date on each so you can collect them in individual student folders. These become performance assessments that will show learning progressions through the semester or year.
- Collect the notes at the door or post them on a Parking Lot.
- Review the notes and start the following class with what has been compiled.

The Exit Pass or Exit Slip strategy is a written form of consolidation of knowledge to assess individual student learning. Students reflect on their learning and summarize it. You are offering ELs and other struggling writers the opportunity to practice their writing skills where they can use the new vocabulary and grammar structures to express their content knowledge.

Questions and Topics for Discussion

1. Why do schools and classrooms need to be permeated with cooperative learning activities?

2. How would you incorporate cooperative learning and classroom management strategies in the SIP's professional development program to prevent LT-ELs?

3. What are the implications from this chapter for your district or your school?

4. How would you take these ideas to another level?

9 Race to the Top

What Administrators Need to Do

Schools are busy places. Decisions we make on a daily basis are part of an integrated, holistic system all centered on student learning. Our focus is on what to teach, how to teach it, how to meet individual student needs, for example, how to meet the language and academic needs of LT-ELs, and how to be confident that these strategies are working. SIPs have a clear and focused purpose: to improve student achievement by increasing the knowledge and skills of educators.

Essential Questions

- What is our school doing to serve LT-ELs?

- How do we teach ELs so that they learn?

- What does a professional development plan look like?

CREATING CHANGE IN SCHOOLS WITH LT-ELS

At the cornerstone of change lays organizational development and its implications on structural systems as well as the necessity for professional development support systems. As the school improvement planning process focuses on increasing student achievement, the principal evaluates the professional development needs of the staff, provides capacity building, implements reform initiatives with appropriate use of resources, and continues to monitor the process. Learning English and the academic content constitutes an interwoven building process and demands a long-term commitment on the part of the school and district.

Align the SIP process with effective quality professional development to teach ELs and all students.

Professional development for teachers of ELs is long-term, sustained and continuous. Unfortunately, some SIPs still reflect traditional forms of professional development and continue to be implemented in some schools. Those forms of professional development are decontextualized one-shot deal workshops presented by external experts, by the "guru of the day," with no chance for application in the classroom and no room at all for application in classrooms with ELs.

Common Findings in Successful Schools

Form a successful professional learning community.

Focus on student work through assessment.

Change their instructional practice accordingly to get better results.

Do all this on a continuing basis.

(Fullan, 2010)

Successful professional development for teachers of ELs includes differentiation strategies to meet the specific linguistic and academic needs of ELs. It also includes coaching on an ongoing basis—classroom observations, debriefings, modeling, coplanning, coteaching, team teaching, peer observation, and debriefing. In other words, teachers will be successful if they answer the key question: *Is my teaching reaching ELs?*

How Do I Incorporate and Implement the ExC-ELL Instructional Components at My School?

First, let's keep in mind that an "everything agenda" school drains all our energy and leaves us tired, frustrated, and empty because we can never fully accomplish what we hope to do.

Second, the SIP is not a school operation plan. At the heart of the SIP is a planned upgrade for professional development the school is committing itself to do for the year, with expansions for the following years. The school changes from "business as usual" to a continuous improvement mindset.

Often, the tendency is to attempt to incorporate many professional development models, or selected strategies and activities in a SIP that are in conflict with each other. Let's consider carefully what can be accomplished in a quality way to teach and reach students. The ExC-ELL model with milestones of implementation of selected research-based strategies can be incorporated. In this way, a focused SIP, including a set of powerful strategies during the first part of the school year and another selection that is added in the second part of the school year and in the ensuing years of ExC-ELL implementation, can turn an "everything agenda" into a "student-long-term-EL achievement" agenda.

> School or district improvement is the mobilization of knowledge, skill, incentives, resources, and capacities within schools and school systems to increase student learning by sharing a set of proven practices and their collective deployment for a common end.
>
> (Elmore, 2008, p. 103)

What Does a District Improvement Plan Look Like?

State education departments across the country have identified Partner Districts and targeted them for intense support and monitoring. The districts are identified as being in Year 3 and beyond in need of whole district improvement based on the state-mandated test results. These districts must develop a District Improvement Plan (DIP) that is then approved by the State Board of Education. Consultants from the departments of education help facilitate the development of the DIP; they also assume a monitoring role upon implementation of the plan. Since there is a great deal of press around the sanctions levied against the targeted district, the DIP development and implementation process must be conducted in a transparent atmosphere with a great deal of public scrutiny. If adequate progress is not shown after the DIP is implemented, the State Board of Education can choose from many sanctions, including, but not limited to, directing the use of funds, mandating the use of specific curricula, and/or state takeover of the district.

Districts are required to engage in a form of improvement planning that differs from historical strategic planning efforts in several ways. DIPs must include research-based, data-driven strategies. Districts should establish no more than three to five goals and limit the strategies committed to in their DIPs.

A DIP that is developed and approved by the state education agency includes evidence of the following required components:

☐ The plan is based on an analysis of data of the whole district and subgroups.
☐ There are no more than three to five goals that are specific, measurable, and defined in terms of student achievement.
☐ There are targets for each subgroup of students identified as being in need of improvement (e.g., LT-ELs, SIFE, special education, African American, Latino, gifted).

☐ The plan incorporates scientifically research-based and data-driven strategies (e.g., vocabulary development, paired reading for ELs, academic writing).

☐ The plan clearly reflects how, when, and by whom implementation of strategies will be monitored and measured.

☐ The plan clearly reflects how, when, and by whom impact of strategies on student achievement will be monitored and measured (e.g., monthly benchmarks, use of the EOP to measure teacher instructional repertoire and its impact on all students).

☐ The plan addresses the fundamental teaching and learning needs in the schools (i.e., after an observation documented with the EOP, the professional development needs are determined as well as the additional support that students will need).

☐ The plan addresses the fundamental teaching and learning needs of specific academic problems of low achieving students (e.g., differentiating for SIFE, LT-ELs, reclassified ELs).

☐ The plan addresses the professional development needs of instructional staff (e.g., teachers for RIGOR, teachers for ExC-ELL; bilingual instructional skills).

☐ The plan includes a commitment to spend the percentage of Title I funds on professional development that is commiserate with the percentage of ELs in that school (applies only to Title I schools/districts).

☐ Professional development is highly focused and aligned to goals and strategies, and the targeted audience is identified (e.g., math teachers need specific adaptations for their ExC-ELL lessons; science experiments will require vocabulary building at different intervals).

☐ The plan specifies the responsibilities of the state and district, including technical assistance.

☐ The plan includes costs of strategies and identifies funding sources.

INTEGRATING ELS INTO YOUR PLANS

In order to create the change you wish to create, it will also be vital for the district administration and the state's administration to be active participants and well-informed supporters of the what, why, and how of your changes. The more knowledgeable they are of the research, evidence, and ways that support systems work for these purposes, the easier your task becomes.

In order to accomplish all this, the first step is for all school personnel to begin participating in extensive professional development on evidenced-based research and practices for ELs and for there to be a parallel strand on creating change in schools. The strand which we'll call "Creating Change for Excellent ELs" is necessary in order for participants to accept and create the changes that help you attain collective goals. In mainstream education, Fullan (2001), Alliance for Excellent Education (2003), Joyce and Showers (2003), and others point to professional development as the cornerstone of capacity building.

The Theory of Action Begins With the "What"

- What do we need to know about our ELs?
- What programs or instructional practices are really evidence-based?
- What are some exemplary cases that we can study and/or visit?
- What tools keep us on track or help us adjust as needed?

These questions are best addressed in Teacher Learning Communities where teachers, site administrators, and literacy/content coaches become learners and peer teachers throughout the study period (Barth, 1990, 2006). The content for the study group targets the various components that will be explored.

Content of Collegial Study on ELs

- Assessments to determine EL programs and assessments bound to EL instruction
- Evidence-based program designs (e.g., SEI, TBE, ESL/sheltered, DL, TWBI, and programs for general education, content teachers, and coaches)
- Evidence-based language, literacy and content instructional strategies and relevant curriculum and materials, aligned with state standards.
- Parental support systems
- The process of professional development (including coaching, Teacher Learning Communities, and other follow-up activities during the year)
- The content of professional development
- Timelines

Enthusiastic educators like to see results or to move as quickly as possible. Successful schools report that intensive collegial study, coupled with initial development of the six components (e.g., professional development content, EL assessments, curriculum and materials, etc.), help participants stay on focus, build positive collegial relationships, build knowledge, and establish a firm foundation for their efforts.

> Each team or partnership in the school becomes responsible for one of the themes. They conduct searches, bring cutting-edge information, and present to the whole group for discussion and implications for implementation.

Knowledge of Our ELs

One of the first things to study is the range of EL's language, literacy, and content knowledge backgrounds in the school and to forecast demographics for the next three years. This facilitates identification of all components and features of the programs to be selected.

We need to know (a) their vocabulary bank in English and in their primary language and degree of academic language, (b) their reading level in English and in their primary language, and (c) their knowledge and application of grammar and writing. If we only test language, we do not get a full picture. A better assessment process will help us select the following:

- The programs to address the diversity of student needs
- The teachers to hire or specific professional development programs to offer
- The configurations of the classrooms per grade level
- The curriculum, textbook levels, and ancillary materials to purchase

Chapter 2 contains graphic organizers that can be used to map out (a) the range of ELs and the type of intervention each might need, (b) a profile of the class, and/or (c) individual student profiles. Forms such as those found in Figures 2.1 and 2.2 can be used to build a profile of a student or a group of ELs. The profiles can give quick glimpses of the numbers and types of students to be placed in different classes. Additionally, it helps a school identify the interventions for SIFE, highly schooled Newcomers, LT-ELs, SE-ELs, or ELs in mainstream classes.

Evidence-Based Program Designs (e.g., SEI, TBE, ESL/sheltered, DL, TWBI)

There are many programs that call themselves "research-based" programs. Unfortunately, even though these programs were based on prior research findings, they have not been empirically tested with ELs and they do not have the evidence to prove their effectiveness with ELs. You want to look for and study programs that have been tested with large enough groups of ELs, at the particular grade level you are interested in addressing. If a program is evidence-based for early grades, this will not help your adolescent ELs, and neither will programs for mainstream, regular teachers.

Evidence-Based Language, Literacy, and Content Instructional Strategies, Relevant Curriculum and Materials, Aligned With State Standards

For ELs, a basic literacy foundation is not enough. They need to extend that basic proficiency in reading into the areas of critical thinking, effective oral and written academic communication, and mastery of new technologies, among other skills. The report *Time to Act* by the Carnegie Council on Advancing Adolescent Literacy (2010) contends that literacy demands change and intensify quickly after fourth grade. Secondary grade students are expected to learn new words, new facts, and new ideas from reading, as well as to interpret, critique, and summarize the content texts they read. The literacy practices require a high level of sophistication, making adolescents vulnerable to underperformance and failure.

> LT-ELs need systematic support to learn how to "read to learn" across a wide variety of contexts and contents.
>
> (Carnegie Council on Advancing Adolescent Literacy, 2010 , p. 10)

Parental Support Systems

States require that districts engage in a form of improvement planning that differs from historical strategic planning efforts in several ways. Districts are legally required to include parents in both the planning and decision-making processes of the district, and the school district must include *professional development training for all teachers on how to actively engage parents in the educational process*. The SIPs require school leaders and teachers to do the following:

- Engage the families and the communities of its students
- Involve parents of ELs as equal partners in the betterment of the school
- Relate to their linguistics needs and strengths and help them become advocates of their children's success in school
- Offer parents training and assistance to become the primary teachers of their children and partners in the life of the school
- Make positive connections between the home and the community experiences of ELs and the core standards

The Process of Professional Development (Including Coaching, Teacher Learning Communities, and Other Follow-Up Activities During the Year)

Educating the full range of ELs and low achieving students in intellectually demanding programs will require education professionals to learn new ways of teaching, with a focus on reading in the content areas. Ongoing professional development for all staff needs to be comprehensive and systematic, with extensive initial institutes followed by other activities based in schools and linked to the instructional program for students. Teachers need theory, research, modeling, or demonstrations of instructional methods, coaching during practice, and feedback in order to integrate instructional practices into their active teaching repertoire (Calderón, 2007; Joyce & Showers, 1983). A teacher-oriented program would provide low-risk practice sessions in a workshop setting where teachers can practice teaching strategies in small teams (Calderón, 1994). Teacher Learning Communities are an integral part of the professional development program and sustain what teachers learn at the training.

Teacher Learning Communities Need to Be

- Structured by specific agendas generated by teachers

- Brief—5 minutes for sharing successes, 5 minutes for problem solving, 10 minutes for instructional demos, 10 minutes for analyzing student work, 5 minutes for celebration

- Scheduled as part of the school's calendar, and time allocated during the workday

(Calderón, 2007, p. 122)

The Content of Professional Development

The initial training requires a framework for improving achievement to meet core standards, to train quality teachers on literacy across the content areas. The ExC-ELL Model uses a research-based design focus. It consists of instructional and professional development combinations for addressing students' and teachers' needs. The ensuing chapters address strategies to build academic vocabulary to comprehend grade-level texts, to engage students with the content area texts, to teach the different writing genre required by each area, and ways to anchor knowledge and skills.

Timelines

The theory of action has begun with the "what"—Its timelines include much preliminary work for a sustained effort reflected in the SIP. It also encompasses an implementation plan of action to accomplish change.

The Next Part of a Theory of Action Is the "How"

- How do I start the change process?
- How do I know our students' backgrounds?
- How do we plan our professional development?

Meaningful school improvement plans specify mutual commitments between actors at different levels (e.g., the principal provides time and coaching for teachers; teachers improve specific skills and knowledge in the course of a school year; the literacy coaches learn how to coach teachers of ELs; the principal and teachers engage in monthly data collection on teacher and student progress). They should also specify measurable benchmarks and accountability for achievement of the goals within the Action Plan.

Checklist to Determine What Is in Place for Second Language, Reading Development, and Content Learning

☐ Appropriate programs are offered to address the range of ELs in the school.

☐ ELs have been appropriately identified and assessed to determine if it is a matter of interrupted education, refinement of reading skills, language development, or a learning disability.

☐ Programs require vocabulary building in English from the early grades and from the beginning of the school year to accelerate learning English and subject matter and to complement vocabulary learning in the first language if it's a DL program.

☐ Programs requires ELs to learn to read in the first language and English simultaneously (during different times of the day) to increase reading achievement in comparison with learning to read in ono language only.

☐ DL and TWBI programs require word reading, phonological awareness, spelling, reading comprehension skills, cognates, syntax and vocabulary development, and concepts in math, science, and social studies to accelerate learning in both languages.

☐ ELs in TBE programs develop reading, language arts, math, science, and social studies knowledge and skills to high levels in order for them to transfer this knowledge and skills into English.

☐ All teachers modify instruction yet maintain rigor.

☐ All teachers create situations for active learning where students are producing rather than "being exposed to" language, reading, and information.

☐ Our technology, curriculum, and materials dovetail with our interventions and our theory of change.

☐ Our professional development dovetails with our interventions and our theory of change.

Evidence-Based Programs and Instructional Practices That Help Make Necessary Changes

The first change is to create design principles and ways of reconciling fidelity of implementation with flexibility of classroom interventions. Which of the changes in Table 9.1 are necessary in your school for second language, reading development, and content learning?

Table 9.1 Program Assumptions and Design Principles	
Assumptions	*Interventions*
1. Appropriate programs are offered to address the diverse backgrounds of ELs.	1. ELs are assessed for placement in the intervention/program that best meets their individual needs.
2. EL programs are comprehensible and schoolwide.	2. There are programs for LT-ELs, SIFE, special education ELs, and reclassified former ELs.
3. EL instruction is based on evidence that it works for them.	3. The programs we have selected for each cohort of ELs have empirical research to support their effectiveness.
4. All their teachers know how to provide effective instruction and are sensitive to their cultural and background knowledge.	4. Teachers working with LT-ELs, SIFE, special education ELs, and reclassified/former ELs know which instructional strategies work best for the group they teach and capitalize on their cultural and background knowledge.
5. Vital participation from school, district, and state administrators is in place.	5. The school, district, and state administration are actively participating and supporting our efforts.
6. ELs know you care for them.	6. Special messages, events, and everyday actions by all adults show they care.
7. You are not afraid to take that first step.	7. Every adult in this school is ready to tackle the changes.

Checklist to Determine Changes Needed

☐ ELs are assessed for placement in the intervention/program that best meets their individual needs.

☐ There are programs for LT-ELs, SIFE, SE-ELs, and reclassified/former ELs.

☐ The programs we have selected for each cohort of ELs have empirical research to support their effectiveness.

☐ Teachers working with LT-ELs, SIFE, SE-ELs, and reclassified/former ELs know which instructional strategies work best for the group they teach and capitalize on their cultural and background knowledge.

☐ The school, district, and state administration are actively participating and supporting our efforts.

☐ Special messages, events, and everyday actions by all adults show they care.

☐ Every adult in this school is ready to tackle the changes.

Questions and Topics for Discussion

1. In what ways does your DIP fulfill its commitment to quality professional development to prevent LT-ELs?
2. What does your SIP's professional development program look like in regard to preventing LT-ELs?
3. What are the implications from this chapter for your district and your school?
4. What would you need to take these ideas to another level?

10

How a Middle School Went From Reconstituted to Highest Performing in Two Years

A Principal's Perspective

By Ysidro Abreu, Guest Author

Middle schools in the United States oftentimes are a fun place to be a principal. There are challenges and rewards that are everlasting for teachers, parents, administrators, and more importantly for students. However, in the United States, performance of middle school students has become a concern. New York's recent Blueprint for Reform document has pointed out the low academic performance of its fourth-, eighth-, and twelfth-grade students and the need to improve their literacy and numeracy skills. Also, as it happens everywhere in the nation, excellence in achievement outcomes for minorities continues to elude the state and the achievement gap between whites and the subgroups of African Americans and Hispanics continues (National Center for Education Statistics, 2009; Sparks, 2009). When comparing Hispanic scores to white scores, little measurable difference has surfaced between 1992 and 2007 (National Center for Education Statistics, 2007).

My reality and goal in middle school is to continue to make faster and more quantifiable efforts to make education a true social equalizer. I also need to continue to address the additional challenge of educating middle school students during a period of adolescence shadowed by myriad physical, social, intellectual, and emotional changes through instruction or other interventions.

I am in my fifth year as a reformer of middle schools. I have been looking for ways to bring to this urban school the ingredients for student achievement and success. It is important to define success not only academically but also emotionally and socially. This school, with more than 95% of Title 1 students and 60% ELs or former ELs, requires great teaching strategies for students to make quantifiable learning gains. For most of these ELs, their first language is Spanish. The school is located in the same neighborhood that I grew up in as an immigrant. These students are my passion.

I founded this middle school when the state's new reform for education began in 2004. The school contains Grades 6 through 8 and has close to 500 students. Since its inception, we have been making great progress with students in the areas of math and literacy. For the last two years, our has received the accolade of "High Performing," "Successful," or an "A" by the district. Math and literacy scores continue to rise compared to scores in similar schools in the district. We do not claim to be the top school, but this high ranking energizes us to work harder so that *all* middle school students meet core state standards and pass the tests.

There are many challenges that we face but language competency is one of the major challenges. Our neighborhood is blessed with continuing traditions, culture, and language. This means that oftentimes the language spoken at home is Spanish. Our students are conflicted concerning when to use the language due to pressures of various kinds, for example, economic, administrative, cultural, political, and religious, which may influence them to use their first language rather than the other. Most of the time, many of our students speak Spanish in the neighborhood; many of the Tier 2, academic words that are essential to enhance content area comprehension are learned in Spanish, and when they are translated into English by our students, they are mainly represented by the word *"Thing."*

The high stakes tests and content area reading require a great amount of vocabulary in English. This creates a problem for our students' reading comprehension and their ability to read to learn. The close relationship between comprehension and vocabulary that occurs during reading stifles or enhances student success (Carnegie Council on Advancing Adolescent Literacy, 2010). Success in middle school ensures that our students achieve & graduate from high school. Students have to learn approximately 2,700 to 3,000 new words per year (Beck, McKeown, & Kucan, 2002; Nagy & Herman, 1987). This translates to an average of 40,000 to 50,000 when they are seniors in high school. For middle school, this translates into approximately seven new words per day per subject area. This fact was one of the many challenges that the school faced and for which I had to find a solution. As part of the solution, we needed to know which programs or strategies were matches for our students. Beck et al. (2002, 2005) and others have highlighted four areas that need to be addressed when helping students learn vocabulary:

1. The first point refers to vocabulary development by wide reading (Nagy & Herman, 1987).

2. Students benefit from direct instruction in vocabulary (Beck, McKeown, & Omanson, 1987; Graves, 1986; Stahl & Fairbanks, 1986).

3. Students can be distracted or hindered as much as they can be helped by context; therefore, use of the dictionary as a strategic tool in acquiring words and meaning is important but only one step in the process of mastering a word (Calderón, 2007).

4. Students can learn some words from context but need instruction about context to be able to use it as an aid.

We struggled with this challenge for two years and tried to address it in different ways. It was during our second year as a school that the district's EL department presented us with an opportunity to embark upon a new program called Expediting Comprehension for English Language Learners (ExC-ELL). ExC-ELL emphasizes the teaching of vocabulary as an integral part of reading comprehension. At first we were skeptical that this type of program could exist, but after meeting with Dr. Calderón and her team, and after attending the professional development institutes, we found that ExC-ELL met the four criteria we espoused and that it was a perfect match for our school. This program has helped our students make academic progress in all subjects year after year. Our reading scores improved in two consecutive years to 45% growth in Levels 3 and 4 (state standard), making the majority of our learners (LT-ELs, SIFE, SE-ELs, and Newcomers) reach at or above grade level in reading.

UNDERSTANDING EXC-ELL FROM THE ADMINISTRATIVE POINT OF VIEW

We found that ExC-ELL's research-based methodologies were a systemic way of teaching vocabulary to *all* learners, not only the English learners. There are five basic components that teachers have to follow in order to teach vocabulary: (a) vocabulary component, (b) oral component, (c) reading component, (d) writing, and (e) classroom context. This program requires staff development for administrators and teachers. Yes! I went through the complete training during the first year of ExC-ELL implementation.

The ExC-ELL program provides an observational rubric which details step by step the necessary instruction and student behavior during vocabulary teaching that are necessary for vocabulary acquisition, reading, oracy, and cooperative learning. The program highlights student application and practice, collaborative work, and the use of definitions by the dictionary as well as student-friendly ones; but most important, it provides strategies on how to teach vocabulary in the context of reading and writing. During our third year using ExC-ELL, a technology component was also added: the use of a digital pen for teachers to observe each other and discuss lessons to improve their teaching.

One of the advantages of this program is the potential to develop a sustained learning culture in schools. This culture can be described as the shared values, beliefs, and orientation that make the members of the organization feel like one, cohesive group and gives them a sense of focus to achieve goals and stay committed. The use of a same language to discuss vocabulary, academic language, literacy and content, and systems to incorporate programs into place are essential for any program to reach the classroom and positively influence our students' learning. ExC-ELL strategies are structured in this manner. Every classroom utilizes artifacts and systems in a systemic way to teach vocabulary. In this manner, the notion of classroom doors closed and isolated from each other is not an alternative. Teachers in all content areas and across grade levels communicate using the same language: cognates, homophones, Tier 2 words, Tier 3 words, and so forth. These aspects are present not only in the teaching but also in every classroom. This gives the school the opportunity to move in the same direction and the ability to reflect in a concerted effort on what needs to be done, what is working, what is not working, and how to improve it.

The latter description provides an example of what Michael Fullan calls "practical theory: Our whole effort is not about discussing change but about getting into it." (2010, p. 4). Because we do all our work in teams, working together is more important than managing up. In this way, I do not have to engineer everything in advance. My role is to harness the power of peers to produce quality change in student teaching and achievement, and in doing so, I build capacity (DuFour, DuFour, Eaker, & Karhanek, 2010).

ExC-ELL provides teachers a way to promote student engagement and incorporate cooperative learning in the classrooms in a schoolwide manner (Carnegie Corporation of New York, 1998). This helps to develop the students' awareness and interest in words, which in turn helps them to develop ownership of these academic words. This is a result of students using the words and understanding how these words are interrelated, as suggested by Beck et al. (2002, 2005).

VALUE-ADDED RESULTS THROUGH THE EXC-ELL PROGRAM

The implementation of ExC-ELL requires that every participant understands the program. It is essential that administrators be trained to make their classroom visitations meaningful for all parties involved. This requires that supervisors be trained prior to implementing the program. Supervisors are helped to understand the theory behind the steps to teach integrated vocabulary, reading, and content, and the rubric/protocol to evaluate teaching strategies and how to create ample opportunities of utilizing the words by all learners and not just a few. This begins to create a clear vision of the instruction and collective capacity that is important for everyone in the organization. Now, there is no more uncertainty of what to do in teaching.

Teachers are trained for five days prior to beginning the program and the school year. This is an essential factor. The training consists of learning the program, practicing the program, and practicing the protocols for coaching. The combination of training with coaching in the school ensures that teachers are supported in the implementation. It gives teachers the opportunity to ask the trainers questions, to observe demo lessons, and to improve the implementation of the program.

As the program becomes part of the school, some teachers begin to emerge as leaders and coaches in their grades and content areas. They identify the ExC-ELL strategies to be implemented and work in concert. This value-added result helps to create a culture of learning for all staff members that greatly accelerates the pace of progress.

The school's schedule must be flexible and supportive to implement ExC-ELL effectively. This program requires the ExC-ELL coaches and/or the school-based coaches to meet with teachers to discuss lessons and plan lessons prior to observation or demo lessons as well as after observations. These evaluations from teacher to teacher or coach to teacher or vice versa are nonevaluative but clinical, constructive feedback. This means that the observations based on the ExC-ELL protocol are utilized only to see how to increase the presence of any of the vital elements in a lesson. The district's Blueprint for Reform document describes this need as one of the five elements that are present in effective middle schools—school structures that are supportive to learning. In our school, teachers have as part of their teaching program a period for study group as well as a period for team meeting. We call this a TLC (Teacher Learning Community). During the period of study group, all teachers in the same content area meet to study a topic or explore implementation and bring student work to discuss next steps as a department and per grade level. During team meetings, the school is divided into smaller TLCs in which all participants of minischools discuss instructional issues, managerial issues, or other important issues to make our school successful. In other words, this gives the opportunity for all members of the school to discuss summative evaluation of the program, which is an important ingredient to successful implementation of any program (Fullan, 2010). In addition, it provides an opportunity to calibrate substantive changes with symbolic interpretations by the school community. This gives the school community the ability to address issues smoothly and rapidly.

Teacher visitations are aided by a computer pen and special paper that captures teacher observations and is sent to a computer which quantifies the teaching numerically. This is performed in a 0–100% utilization of the strategies and is represented in bar graphs that can be utilized for further discussion for teacher to teacher or for supervisor to teacher reflection and feedback.

COOPERATIVE LEARNING

Oftentimes cooperative learning in middle schools means that a group of students sit together and everyone is given a role. This role of cooperative groups had to be changed at our school when we began to implement ExC-ELL. The ExC-ELL program counts heavily on utilizing hands-on activities in which all learners participate utilizing, thinking, and making sense of the vocabulary and text being read. Keeping students on task, not given roles, avoids classroom management problems and promotes a positive school climate. Students participate 100% during the activity; they are accountable and responsible for learning. For example, all learners produce a final product based on different active work of different learners in the group. If they are writing a paragraph utilizing a main idea, all learners must create a main idea and then discuss which is the best main idea or create a main idea which has all the major ingredients of the main ideas created by all the group members. This provides all learners the opportunity to acquire the concept. All learners use the vocabulary, write sentences with the vocabulary, and use context clues to infer new vocabulary meaning. We have adapted this type of cooperative groups in all subjects. For example, in math, prior to finding the function that describes a pattern, students must think independently and look at the facts to come up with a function or set of facts, and then with sticky notes, they place each individual response on group chart paper and begin to create a final product. With this process, each student is able to probe others' thinking and create meaning to acquire the concept. This type of cooperative learning ensures that all children are truly participants of the learning process.

CONTENT AREA TEACHERS TEACHING VOCABULARY

If you ask a middle school teacher who does not have a literacy or reading license how to teach vocabulary or language, he might feel a sense of discomfort. As a former math teacher, I had to teach math vocabulary, but I didn't know why students came to my classroom without prior knowledge of some of the prerequisite math vocabulary from their elementary school. The more one becomes experienced in teaching, one begins to understand the difference between teaching and learning. One can teach all one wants to students, but what the student learns is a different story. The use of Tier 3 words as part of students' academic language is extremely important. In order for students to be able to comprehend content area, material vocabulary development is extremely important—especially at our school in which a great number of students are former or ELs. Cummins (1984) explains that it could take about seven years for ELs to develop the appropriate level of academic proficiency. However, this does not have to be the case. One of the main reasons why academic conversational skills are acquired more easily is because conversations occur in context-embedded opportunities. ExC-ELL utilizes this strategy of context-embedded opportunities to teach discourse. The same way that vocabulary is addressed in a literacy class is utilized to address the Tier 3 words in all subjects. The utilization of ExC-ELL in all subject areas gives us the opportunity to ensure that our students are prepared to go to high school with the necessary vocabulary to succeed. We have extended the use of vocabulary in our content areas in the use of math journals, discussion circles, word banks, word walls, and many other activities. This provides students with the opportunity to improve their ability to construct meaning and not just learn isolated words. These initiatives as value added to ExC-ELL provide students with the opportunity to own the words and be interested in learning the words.

A CULTURE OF A SCHOOL UTILIZING EXC-ELL

Although we have three years utilizing ExC-ELL in our school, we are still developing the next steps. First, we began with the ESL teachers and literacy teachers and have gradually embarked in all subject areas. At this point, we have been able to identify an internal teacher who has become our ExC-ELL leader who works with and supports teachers within the school community.

When you walk around a school in which ExC-ELL is utilized, you will find the following elements: Inside the classrooms there are walls for Tier 1, 2, and 3 words, polysemous words, and lists of cognates. The use of multiple-meaning words is evident. Lessons have a precise way of being executed with steps to follow, and from classroom to classroom, teaching vocabulary occurs in the same manner. Students are reading, involved, and working cooperatively. The teachers are modeling reading strategies and assessing the use of those comprehension strategies during partner reading, and the learning and acquisition of vocabulary occurs in every lesson. You might find teachers discussing a lesson plan. One teacher from the ESL department might be helping the science teacher develop an activity that utilizes ExC-ELL Tier 3 words. One might also find teachers observing each other during their preparatory periods and discussing their observations utilizing the computer pen printouts or ExC-ELL protocol. You might walk into a math class and find students writing in their math journals utilizing the learned vocabulary and a highlighter pen, underlining the vocabulary words taken from the lesson or previous lessons. Once the school has developed fidelity to the program and has learned the foundation of the program, there are ways in which to adapt school initiatives to ExC-ELL in order for them to coexist and not to become competitive or divisive among implementers.

In order for the ExC-ELL program to flourish in a school community, it needs commitment and support. The results from that commitment are not only better students outcomes but better flexible scheduling, more opportunities for learning, and the development of expert teachers and teachers who have a greater influence in their classrooms and comprehensive approach to teach language, literacy, and the subject domains in the middle school.

Letter From Principal or Administrator to Communicate With Teachers After a Visit by a Consultant

If there is a need for teaching strategies or instructional school initiatives to thrive in order to affect student performance and become part of the school culture, the leader of the school community has to be a motivator. One cannot be an effective principal without knowing how to motivate followers (Elmore, 2008, 2009; Guthrie & Reed, 1991). It is important for the school community to know how much the leader cares. Jazzar and Algozzine (2005) explain that leaders know that others don't care how much leaders know, until others know how much leaders care! It is necessary to motivate staff and care about results in order for a school culture to embrace and own a program or teaching strategy. Guthrie and Reed (1991) divided effective motivation into three principles: Inspire by example, inspire by goal elevation, and inspire by co-option. Therefore, I sent letters to each teacher after each visit, highlighting all the positive things I had observed as well as a recommendation for next steps.

Another aspect that is essential to create an ExC-ELL culture is the empowerment of some individuals or resulting leaders from the program. The empowerment of teachers gives a sense of togetherness or teamwork and helps the organization and school community to be shaped by all members. Empowerment emphasizes shared leadership, participative decision making, mutual trust, supportive relationships, and quality of work life.

There are some steps that were taken into account to embrace ExC-ELL in our school. We found it necessary to do the following:

- Identify roles and responsibility with the school team working with ExC-ELL (vital component).
- Establish checkpoints with teachers on trainers' and coaches' performance:
  o Ask teachers what is working or not working with coaches or trainers.
  o Ask teachers what are some strategies or barriers that the coaches' style might bring to the process.
  o Ask teachers what is needed for coaches to be more effective.

- Highlight effective teacher and application strategies:
  o Have teachers demonstrate to others.
  o Highlight practices and ask teachers to visit each other.

- Establish school program structures during the school day for shared learning:
  - Teacher Learning Communities should take place during school.
  - Afterschool staff development or planning should be part of the school budget.

- Develop plans for collegial support:
  - Allow time during the day for teachers to observe each other and plan lessons.
  - Allow time for debriefing with coaches and colleagues in grade level and schoolwide.

- Determine next steps for continuous improvement:
  - Discuss next steps with coaches and teachers.
  - Look at student work.

The principal should also be part of this process. It's necessary to be an implementer and understand the program. An effective principal must also extend his or her role as principal to be one of an instructional leader and to seek opportunities to advise and counsel others in need.

CREATING AN EXC-ELL MIDDLE SCHOOL ATMOSPHERE

Informing the Staff

Prior to implementation, the principal and/or ExC-ELL team should emphasize two major goals targeted to infuse good teaching practices for language and literacy and a collegial atmosphere into the school culture:

ExC-ELL is a program that enriches student opportunity to have access to content area materials. It is full of great teaching experiences, but it is a goal winner when it comes to systemic implementation of routines and rituals of what teaching strategies to utilize and what students should accomplish.

The ExC-ELL program always involves a self -question: *Is my teaching reaching?* Therefore, it takes a community of learners and leaders to enforce this set of strategies, rituals, and routines to have fidelity to the program. In order to "excel," participants have to be assisted with feedback, as well as opportunities to observe and apply the ExC-ELL protocol as a foundation to assure that the community teaching is reaching.

Communicating the Need

As founder of a middle school in which 66% are ELs or former ELs, I have developed a passion for this program, which is promoting accessibility of language to our students. In this endeavor, we scaffolded the implementation. Year 1 and 2 teachers were trained in a summer institute. It was obvious that if we wanted ExC-ELL to become an intrinsic component of our middle school's instructional life, there was a need to involve the assistant principals and coaches of all subjects (math, science, social studies, literacy, ESL, and bilingual Spanish). To truly support the community of teachers, we observed teachers with the ExC-ELL trainers and participated in follow-up up discussions, ensuring that the necessary components will be addressed in the future, further ensuring growth in the teachers' professional development.

Speaking the Same Language

No one in our school community can claim misunderstandings due to the protocol and clear program steps. The language that we use to discuss the growth in application of ExC-ELL is based on preobservation and postobservation protocol data.

As we entered our third year, I felt that another layer of discussion needed to be added in an effort to continue fidelity and our students' academic progress. Using data generated by the computer pen utilized by the ExC-ELL coaches and our coaches, I gave teachers e-mail feedback pointing out a variety of aspects: what is working, the current focus, next steps, and possible support to ensure that the quantitative data from the next round of observations show progress on behalf of teacher performance.

Supportive Environment That Emphasizes Teacher Empowerment and Quality of Work

Our model to ensure fidelity is represented here:

Next Observation looking at → Meeting with teacher to discuss lessons or demo ↓

We are invested in the implementation of ExC-ELL in our school and believe that it is essential that all of the participants develop a sense of ownership and accountability in order to ensure that our teaching is reaching our children.

Questions and Topics for Discussion

1. What are the implications from this principal's perspective for your school? What are the basics for good implementation?

2. What are the changes/refinements in the SIP necessary to incorporate ExC-ELL to teach and reach ELs?

3. How can your school achieve/sustain high performing status?

4. What would take this principal's SIP to another level?

11 Systemic School Reform

Partnering to Ensure EL Success

By Hector Montenegro, EdD,
Guest Author

School reform initiatives come and go, yet the general expectations in education remain the same: to increase graduation rates, close the achievement gap, and improve instruction. Since the early 1960s, hundreds of educational reform strategies have been touted as the answer to all of our academic woes. We have gone from open space education to block scheduling to schools within a school, all with mixed results. The educational buzzwords were once vocational education, career education, and career pathways, but now the emphasis is on college readiness, early college, advanced placement, dual credit, meeting state standards, and global education. The list of new reform initiatives is extensive! However, in spite of these changes, more students live in poverty and are dropping out of school, and the performance gap is widening. In fact, forced desegregation of the 1960s & 1970s, a well-intended but controversial school reform initiative, has taken us from intentional segregation to desegregation and now back to de facto segregated public and charter schools.

Educators have had their hands full over the past 50 years adapting to the barrage of changes in the educational landscape. Once considered a characteristic of the southwest and Florida, the large influx of ELs into our schools is now a national reality. The plight of ELs is of particular importance because they have the highest incidence of poverty, school failure, and underemployment of all other student populations. The inability of school districts to adequately respond to the needs of ELs is due in part to the lack of appropriate training, limited or no understanding of language acquisition models, limited exposure to available instructional resources, inflexible bureaucratic infrastructures, and uninformed administrators.

EDUCATING ELS

Teachers and administrators struggle with educating nontraditional students who enter our schools lacking fluency in English and often in their native language, unfamiliar with the U.S. educational system, and a tendency to isolate themselves in their cultural and language enclaves. The search for best practices and optimal language acquisition models for school districts serving ELs is exceptionally difficult in light of the unpredictable forces that influence demographic changes and the limited organizational capacity to respond to these rapid changes. Some of the challenges that most districts face in addressing the needs of ELs include selecting optimal language acquisition models, fulfilling the need for comprehensive and appropriate professional development, selecting and allocating resources, and assigning highly qualified teachers in classrooms with ELs while facing severe budgetary constraints. This is not a simple process and even school districts that have some of the most comprehensive and longstanding ESL and bilingual programs have not been as successful educating their ELs as one may assume.

In this age of accountability, politically charged English Only movements, and anti-immigrant sentiment, educators are often forced to be in compliance with local, state, and national standards. Even though being in compliance is important, the selection of research-based quality programs that have demonstrated to be most effective in helping ELs become critical thinkers and reach high levels of cognitive development should be of highest priority. As with all students, ELs need to have access to and an opportunity to master the full curriculum in one or more languages. In general, school districts do not have the capacity to select the most appropriate language acquisition models for ELs in all grade levels and who generally have a wide range of language ability. Since no two school districts are identical and the number of ELs in a district varies, instructional models for ELs may differ from school to school and between school districts. Unfortunately, inconsistent and misaligned educational practices in schools that unintentionally impede efforts to close the achievement gap, result in a decrease in graduation rates and generally underserve the needs of an increasing diverse and multilingual student population. There is an absence of a comprehensive and sustainable reform design that can address all of the current educational challenges, especially the needs of ELs.

IN SEARCH OF BEST PRACTICES FOR ELS

Across the country, there are many examples of efforts to address the needs of ELs that vary depending on the student composition and district capacity. My first year as a principal at Hammond Junior High School in Alexandria, Virginia, a suburb of Washington, D.C., was in 1986. Hammond had Grades 7–9 with over 1,200 students, a majority minority population and more than 40 different language groups from Latin America, Asia, Africa, and Middle Eastern countries. This was quite a change from the predominately white, Hispanic, and African American demographic I had experienced prior to coming to Hammond. What made this situation so unique was the rapid and unexpected demographic change. Other than traditional ESL programs, clear guidelines on how best to address the needs of this diverse student population were neither clear nor well defined. There was little diversity among the faculty and staff and neither the school nor district had the language capacity to communicate to all of these 40 language groups and their families. Even though the school had caring and supportive faculty and staff, the language acquisition models were limited and there was little alignment between grade levels and across schools.

In contrast, I later became the superintendent of schools for the Ysleta Independent School District (YISD) in El Paso, Texas, in 2003. YISD consists of 45,000 students where 93% are Hispanic, approximately 23% are ELs, and nearly 50% of the faculty and staff are bilingual (English and Spanish). There had not been a significant demographic shift in decades and the native language of the ELs was valued and respected, making multilingual communications the norm rather than the exception. In spite of the relative homogeneous community, the instructional models for ELs varied from ESL to TBE, DL programs, and even a multilingual immersion program where, in addition to English and Spanish, students also learned a third language before entering high school. Even though there existed many two-way DL programs from K–12, the options for language acquisition models in YISD depended on the grade level, capacity of the administrators and teachers to provide quality instruction, and a rich language learning environment. In spite of differences in program design, most language acquisition models in YISD produced extraordinary results in student performance. Most importantly, well-trained teachers who worked in a collaborative culture made the critical difference in the success or failure of these EL students. As stated in previous chapters, regardless of the program type (e.g., ESL, TBE, DL), what matters most is quality of instruction.

More often than not, the availability of English language models is governed by the capacity and desire of district level personnel to make critical instructional choices that are aligned and address the needs of ELs. The range of demographic diversity in many school districts nationally varies from a few ELs from the same background to a multicultural population that has a wide range of academic levels and psychological needs. This diverse student composition makes the search for best practices particularly difficult in the schools that have not adequately prepared for this influx of Newcomers. Best practices and research-based successful language acquisition models may not always be appropriate for all schools needing intervention strategies for ELs. In developing English language programs that graduate ELs on time and prepares them for a more productive future, all of the components of a district infrastructure, from the classroom to central office, need to be actively engaged in the evaluation and selection process of appropriate language acquisition methodologies, resources, and personnel. Whether ESL, SE, TBE, one-way or two-way DL immersion, or even multilingual programs are best for a school district is a matter of demographics, educational orientation, district capacity, political influences, and budget.

We now have sufficient evidence to know that DL, TWBI, and even TBE programs work. So do structured SEI programs. However, there are reasons other than effects on English reading that a school might prefer to teach in the children's first language: cognitive advantages, academic success, family ties, career advantages, personal well-being, bilingualism (August & Shanahan, 2006; August, Goldenberg, & Rueda, 2010; Calderón & Slavin, 2010). One of the main reasons two-way, DL programs are so successful is because the classes are integrated with EL and English dominant students that learn both languages from the teacher and from each other (August & Shanahan, 2006, 2008; Calderón & Carreón, 1994; Calderón et al., 1998). In effect, ELs in DL programs are not socially segregated, their language is valued, they both have access to peer-level language models that motivate them to develop fluency in the second language, and they become acculturated quicker by having regular social interactions with the culture of their classmates. Calderón's (2007) 12 components for Expediting Comprehension for English Language Learners (ExC-ELL) help teachers in all these types of programs accelerate learning for ELs, and ExC-ELL is a model to be emulated. So why doesn't every school with ELs adopt this instructional model?

ExC-ELL is a model to be emulated. It is comprehensive, inclusive of all stakeholders, collaborative, systemic, data driven, and evidence-based. The use of the EOP is a critical tool used to ensure fidelity of the program by way of observation strategies that help administrators, literacy coaches, and teachers become more reflective of instructional practices. The goal is to increase student learning by enhancing teacher effectiveness that is in line with academic standards, graduation requirements, and district expectations. ELs fail because they are not receiving grade-level content and core standards in rich learning environments with highly prepared teachers (Calderón, 2007). In addition, this may be directly related to the large number of LT-ELs at the secondary level who are born in the United States and have attended public schools for over seven years.

The most critical question that should be asked is this: Why doesn't every school with ELs adopt these evidence-based instructional models? The answer to this question lies in the capacity of a school district to make comprehensive systemic changes that ultimately have a profound impact on the success rate of all children. Unfortunately, inflexible educational bureaucracies may be the culprits behind failed attempts to make significant changes in the instructional process.

CHANGING INFLEXIBLE BUREAUCRACIES

Within educational and community circles, we often hear about the need to change failing and bureaucratic school systems, but we have never been clear as to what needs to be changed, why, and to what? How is school reform defined? Is the latest instructional resource or reform strategy always the best? Educators often get caught up in doing the right thing for the wrong reasons. Since the early 1960s, there has been extensive research on school reform and "Changing the System." Far too often, we have confused the latest ideas, state-of-the-art designs, or even researched-based practices as being synonymous with the best way to educate children. What works in one educational setting may not be appropriate for all, especially if the capacity for full implementation is limited.

Superintendents and educators alike know all too well that inflexible bureaucracies can often be punitive, compliant-driven, and operate from proverbial silos that neither interface nor work in a collaborative environment to respond optimally to unexpected changes in the system. The silo effect exists when campus and central office administrators, faculty and staff, perform their duties in isolation of one another. Random acts of excellence are commonplace in education, but systemic collaborative decision-making strategies that are child-centered and meet the spirit of school or district mission and vision statements are most often nonexistent. Administrators generally are not cognizant of effective change theories and have not developed the skills to create flexible collaborative organizations that can adapt to changing demographics in student populations and generational paradigms.

A fundamental shift in mindset at the administrative level is needed in order to increase the probability of making truly collaborative decisions on program selection, systemic alignment of instructional strategies, fidelity in the implementation of adopted programs, and stakeholder buy-in on all new initiatives. Though there are no guarantees, the goal of this approach is to minimize or eradicate the silos that exist in educational institutions so as to create collaborative cultures that are systemic, intentional in purpose, and produce sustainable results. This framework is at the heart of selecting effective and sustainable English language programs for ELs.

Recently, there have been several attempts to address poor student performance and instructional inconsistencies in schools. Collins's *Good to Great* (2001), DuFour and Eaker's *Professional Learning Communities at Work* (1998), and Fullan's focus on the *Six Secrets of Change* (2008) have all proposed frameworks that address the need for a more interactive and interdependent educational system that produces desired outcomes. Even the No Child Left Behind legislation called for school reform and accountability for all students, especially ELs that were reading below grade level. Unfortunately, systemic school reform is far too often defined by programs that are poorly understood and poorly implemented by middle managers who are poorly trained. This is at the root of many complications related to the implementation of effective bilingual education programs.

We can often learn from some of the most well-intended yet failed school reform initiatives in our educational history. As a first-year teacher intern with the Teacher Corps in 1975, I was led to believe that we were training to become "Agents of Change" in an urban setting. At Herbert Hoover Junior High in the San Jose Unified School district, I taught seventh-grade math in a portable building because they were completing a new open space junior high school that was scheduled to open in the spring of 1976. As a first-year teacher, I was excited that I would be able to experience such a monumental transition to an entirely new way of teaching and managing education. It seemed as if this was the wave of the future and we were at the forefront of a radical departure from the traditional way of educating children.

Once we moved into the new building, inherent problems with the facility design and instructional strategies became painfully obvious. In retrospect, there were many flaws and oversights in the preparation for the transition. I do not recall any practice teaching in a cooperative learning environment, no collaborative lesson planning, no team teaching, no predetermined process to troubleshoot challenges, no agreement on classroom management strategies in an open space environment, and very little consensus on standards for classroom discipline. In effect, it was designed to fail. As was the case for thousands of open space schools around the country, the walls soon went up and teaching went back to the old private way of doing things. To this day, I still draw upon the lessons learned from Herbert Hoover, that is, inflexible bureaucracies tend to permit superficial change but do not restructure to ensure effectiveness and sustainability of educational innovation.

Technology, for example, is another aggressive but poorly planned innovative reform effort. We have gone from the terminals, to computer labs, computers on wheels (COWs), Thin Clients, iPods, and iPads, and now laptops for every child are being used for virtual schools, distance learning, and 24/7 learning opportunities. Though these innovations have provided alternative instructional delivery systems, technology upgrades are frequently driven by the obsession to stay current at all costs without thorough and purposeful staff development that is based on clearly defined goals and expectations. Unfortunately, beyond sporadic anecdotes of success, there is very little evidence that technology is universally used and consistently produces extraordinarily high levels of student achievement.

The transition from theory and design to goals and expectations, implementation and sustainability, is inconsistent, not clearly understood, and often sabotaged by poorly thought out succession practices, political agendas, and a general lack of understanding of aligned systems by administrators and especially central office. Most recently, $4 billion in federal money has been allocated for "Race to the Top" grants that expect applicants to adopt standards and assessments that prepare students to succeed in college and the workplace and to compete in the global economy; build data systems that measure student growth and success and inform teachers and principals how they can improve instruction; recruit, develop, reward, and retain effective teachers and principals, especially where they are needed most; and turn around our lowest achieving schools (U.S. Department of Education, 2010).

This sounds like a perfect formula for a systemic approach to addressing the needs of all students. What is missing are clear guidelines regarding specific behaviors that would ensure success, such as a collective effort to align systems and ensure comprehensive stakeholder buy-in and a commitment from superintendents and school boards for long-term continuity and consistency in program implementation. Most importantly, what is going to happen to these programs once the funding ends? In these bad economic times, superintendents are being forced to revert to draconian measures to keep districts from bankruptcy. This poses serious concerns regarding the continuity and consistency of any new initiative.

The components of a well thought-out instructional infrastructure begin with getting the "right" people in leadership positions who can competently lead the efforts to align curriculum standards, develop a scope and sequence, ensure proper curriculum mapping, inspire active administrative support for instruction, implement formative and summative assessments, utilize disaggregated data to modify instruction, and respond to failure with aggressive intervention strategies. This inclusive model can only be created and sustained if the district leadership understands the dynamics of change and the implications of an "interdependent" organization. This includes mobilizing all of the component parts and de-privatizing the educational enterprise to increase levels of cooperation and collaborative decision making.

A MATTER OF CHOICE AND COMMITMENT

Developing collaborative district infrastructures that make sound programmatic choices and support those choices over time lies at the root of all success stories for educational initiatives. Every school and every school district in the country potentially has the capacity and knowledge to create and sustain successful programs for all ELs. At the heart of this process is the "will and desire" to put children first in all critical decision making. This often means that adults need to eliminate all negative preconceived notions of ELs because of initial language and cultural barriers. Acquiring the tools, resources, and skills necessary to accelerate learning for these children, set high expectations, and prepare them for academic success is a matter of choice and commitment.

Eliminating organizational silos and bureaucratic inflexibilities that block and inhibit teacher and administrative effectiveness should be of highest priority. This can best be achieved by creating and promoting a culture of collaborative decision making based on comprehensive and reliable data. This level of thinking is at the heart of an interdependent systemic approach that puts the goals and vision for all children at the center of all decision making. For example, if ELs are not being successful in transitioning from a sheltered English environment to a more academically rigorous environment, then the data should be studied and modifications made to instruction in order to enhance learning within the context of a content-rich curriculum. Instructional technology should be directly aligned with curriculum and utilized more frequently to enhance

ELs. Exit criteria should be clearly defined and articulated across grades in order to avoid LT-ELs. It is a matter of choice as to whether or not administrators and teachers want to collaborate and spend the time to research and implement the most effective instructional methods, interdisciplinary language acquisition models, and instructional resources available to help ELs accelerate learning. Without a well thought-out change strategy, teacher effectiveness and the quality of instruction will be left to chance. As this book contends, we already know what it takes to educate students well. Now we need the will and commitment to do so on a sustained basis (Edmonds, 1979, 1982; Elmore, 2008; Fullan, 2010; Schmoker, 2006).

At the heart of all systemic school reform are people, people, people! It can't be done without the hearts and minds of those involved in decision making, teaching and administering programs, and creating collaborative cultures that align systems and build capacity to achieve desired goals. But the partnerships need to extend beyond the schoolhouse and district offices. They need to include business partners that will give children the hopes and dreams that will inspire them to attain higher goals for themselves. Unfortunately, the dropout rate for ELs is among the highest in the nation and unless there is immediate and comprehensive intervention, hundreds of thousands of bright, capable students will continue to be underemployed and undereducated, and they will be ill prepared to prevent their children from meeting the same fate.

SYSTEMIC PARTNERSHIPS

Addressing the academic and social needs of all ELs will take a systemic approach very much like what would be necessary for all students in any school district. We know that successful EL programs have infrastructure characteristics and quality teachers common to most successful schools in the country. Therefore, the only way any instructional initiative can be sustained is to build flexible infrastructures that are designed to synchronize people and resources with a common vision for desired outcomes. It is not enough to be in compliance or have all the data needed to analyze and modify instructional practices. What is essential in order for school districts to produce better results for ELs is for the entire system—central office and schools, stakeholders and partners—to work in concert with one another to align strategies and resources and demonstrate a commitment to continuous improvement. Otherwise, we will continue to "chase our tails" and wonder why, with all the hard work and perpetual motion, we are not making any progress.

Questions and Topics for Discussion

1. How would this chapter inform your district's theory of action and change?

2. What are the changes you need to address for the professional development of teachers of ELs at your district?

3. Outline your DIP to reflect teaching and reaching ELs with grade-level content and core standards in rich learning environments with highly prepared teachers. Use the information to share with other stakeholders.

4. What would take this superintendent's DIP to another level?

12 LT-ELs and Core Standards

Myth: The research says that it takes seven or more years to learn English.

Problem: Educators use this as an excuse to let students go from grade to grade without rigorous instruction. We hear teachers and administrators say, "He is only in the fifth grade; he has two or more years to catch up and be reclassified." This is perhaps the biggest excuse that has generated the huge LT-EL population.

Reality: The seven-year myth has never been proven with empirical scientific studies. The studies we shared in this book, and forthcoming studies from other researchers, indicate that students can be proficient in four years in either SEI/SE, TBE/DL, or TWBI programs in elementary schools—if all the 10 features of school success and effective implementation described in Chapter 3 are adhered to with fidelity. Secondary schools can accelerate their learning and academic achievement, even rescue those that are coming in this year as LT-ELs, by adhering to the same features.

Myth: "Push In" and "Pull Out" programs can provide quality instruction for ELs in secondary schools.

Problem: Even when school districts mandate two hours or more of ESL instruction for each student, it is logistically impossible for one ESL teacher to do this while servicing more than three students in one day. "Push In" clocks in 10 or 15 minutes per student per day and entails mostly translating or helping to answer questions, not explicit instruction. "Pull Out" clocks in a little more time, but teachers usually have so many EL levels that instruction entails mostly helping with homework or ESL activities that may or may not be helpful to each student's content load.

Reality: All teachers in middle and high schools have ELs and other students that need more relevant and rigorous instruction. Unless all teachers in a middle and high school receive comprehensive state-of-the art professional development on how to integrate academic vocabulary, reading comprehension, and writing skills development for the courses they teach, there will never be sufficient quality time on instruction for ELs, struggling readers, or special education students.

As a summary of what we have intended to convey in this book, we close with these recommendations, in the hope of dispelling these and many other prevalent myths or clichés (. . . they don't want to go to college . . . they're not interested in school . . . they're shy . . . their parents don't come because they don't care . . .). These recommendations are also for discussion with whole faculties, district administrators, and professional development providers working with your school.

FOR ELEMENTARY SCHOOLS: CLASSROOM INSTRUCTION

- ☐ Teach vocabulary for every subject every day.
- ☐ Teach reading (phonemic awareness, decoding, comprehension skills) within the context of reading language arts, math problems, science, and social studies.
- ☐ Teach writing for the math, science, and social studies genres as well as the language arts genre.
- ☐ Use leveled readers for all subject areas, not just language arts.
- ☐ Use differentiated materials for the tutoring or intensive interventions of each student category (e.g., SIFE, Newcomers, novice, developing, expanding, bridging, former limited English proficient/ reclassified).
- ☐ Integrate ELs with other students without sacrificing comprehension and learning.
- ☐ Use cooperative learning to integrate students, foment cross-cultural relationships, and practice 21st-century skills (e.g., collaboration, higher order thinking, creativity).

☐ Include in all instructional daily lessons the following: vocabulary/discourse objective, reading comprehension objective, core content standard, and how each will be assessed.

☐ If it is a DL program, provide all of the aforementioned items in both languages.

☐ If it is an SEI program, use the *strategic use* of the primary language (e.g., cognates, syntactical differences/similarities), not translation.

☐ Show genuine respect for all cultures; display appreciation for the home culture of your students throughout.

FOR ELEMENTARY SCHOOLS: STRUCTURES, SUPPORT, AND SERVICES

☐ Meet with feeder middle schools and find out how many LT-ELs came from your school.

☐ Identify the conditions that contributed toward creating LT-ELs.

☐ Meet with your feeder preschool and discuss your expectations for their students.

☐ Identify, test, or retest your ELs or possible ELs.

☐ Go back and find all the ELs who have been reclassified or exited from a program. How are they doing?

☐ Identify the teachers who have been adequately trained and those who need more training.

☐ Identify how many teachers need to be hired and the selection criteria for those hires.

☐ Clearly define your program model (SEI, TBE, TWBI) and implementation guidelines (e.g., distribution of languages, team-teaching protocols, expectations).

☐ Align curriculum across grade levels, ensuring consistency and coherence in the alignment with core standards and EL standards.

☐ Publish and discuss expectations of teacher and student growth.

☐ Track and discuss achievement gains for ELs in each category/proficiency level and length of time in your school.

☐ Follow the guidelines for RTI and reassess ELs to determine if it is a language, literacy, or learning intervention that each one needs.

☐ Provide quality intensive language/literacy interventions in after-school, Saturday, or summer programs for students who need extra assistance.

☐ Provide RTI Tier 2 and Tier 3 interventions that are of high quality and assess the programs, the teachers, and the students on a quarterly basis.

☐ Provide differentiated professional development instruction for your K–5 teachers; institute coaching and Teacher Learning Communities.

☐ Monitor implementation through data collection and measure the transfer from training.

☐ Provide fourth- and fifth-grade teachers with extensive professional development instruction on how to provide rigorous challenging instruction in all subjects in a way that prepares students to go into sixth grade without such wide gaps in vocabulary and content knowledge.

☐ Provide professional development instruction for your literacy coaches on EL instruction and what and how to observe and coach teachers with ELs.

☐ Require that all administrators and supervisors also attend professional development programs on EL instruction and school structures and supports.

☐ Monitor teacher quality and fidelity of implementation through data collection, and measure the transfer from training to ascertain if the professional development instruction is functioning or needs readjustment.

☐ Engage EL parents. There are many ways to show them that you care about them and their children.

FOR MIDDLE AND HIGH SCHOOLS: CLASSROOM INSTRUCTION

☐ All teachers of math, science, and social studies preteach vocabulary before students are assigned readings. They model a comprehension strategy that is appropriate to that segment of reading. They model the writing genre to be used for the report/writing assignment.

☐ Teachers use leveled readers for all subject areas if there are different levels of readers or ELs.

☐ ESL teachers address the acceleration of language and literacy learning and use differentiated materials for the intensive interventions of each student category (e.g., SIFE, Newcomers, novice, developing, expanding, bridging, former limited English proficient/reclassified).

☐ ELs are integrated with other students without sacrificing comprehension and learning because all content teachers are adequately trained.

☐ Teachers use cooperative learning to integrate students, foment cross-cultural relationships, apply English discourse, and practice

21st-century skills (e.g., collaboration, higher order thinking, creativity).

☐ Teachers post and discuss with students the daily vocabulary/discourse objective, reading comprehension objective, core content standard, and how each will be assessed.

☐ If it is a DL program, provide all of the aforementioned items in each language of instruction. Foreign language and heritage language teachers also address all of these instructional features.

☐ If it is an SEI program, use the *strategic use* of the primary language (e.g., cognates, syntactical differences/similarities), not translation.

☐ Secondary school teachers show genuine respect for all cultures and display appreciation for the home culture of the students.

FOR MIDDLE AND HIGH SCHOOLS: STRUCTURES, SUPPORT, AND SERVICES

☐ Meet with feeder middle schools and find out how many LT-ELs are coming from their school. Discuss your expectations for their students.

☐ Identify, test, or retest your ELs or possible ELs. Interview them to learn their life and educational histories, their current situation or needs.

☐ Find all the former ELs and determine from their course grades and required exams if they need intensive targeted assistance.

☐ Provide quality intensive language/literacy instruction in all mainstream content classrooms coupled with rigorous interventions in afterschool, Saturday, or summer programs to accelerate learning for LT-ELs.

☐ Clearly define your program model (SEI, TBE, TWBI) and implementation guidelines (e.g., distribution of languages, team-teaching protocols, expectations).

☐ Identify the teachers who have been adequately trained and those who need more training.

☐ Identify how many teachers need to be hired and the selection criteria for those hires.

☐ Ensure consistency and coherence in the core curriculum and electives, and align them with core standards and EL standards.

☐ Follow the guidelines for RTI and reassess ELs to determine if it is a language, literacy, or learning intervention that each one needs.

☐ Publish and discuss expectations of teacher and student growth for each quarter.

☐ Track and discuss achievement gains for ELs in each category/ proficiency level and length of time in your school.

☐ Provide RTI Tier 2 and Tier 3 interventions that are of high quality and assess the programs, the teachers, and the students on a quarterly basis.

☐ Ensure that ELs have access to advanced placement courses, gifted and talented programs, electives, and credits leading to college.

☐ Encourage students through well-trained counselors to prepare for college.

☐ Provide differentiated professional development instruction for content teachers with time to integrate language and literacy into their content lessons; institute coaching and Teacher Learning Communities.

☐ Monitor teacher quality and fidelity of implementation through data collection, and measure the transfer from training to ascertain if the professional development instruction is functioning or needs readjustment.

☐ Ensure that content and ESL/SEI teachers obtain extensive professional development instruction on how to provide rigorous challenging instruction in all subjects.

☐ Provide professional development instruction for your literacy or content coaches on EL instruction and what and how to observe and coach teachers with ELs.

☐ Ensure that all administrators and supervisors also attend professional development programs on EL instruction and school structures and supports.

☐ Engage EL parents. There are many ways to show them that you care about them and their children.

FOR ASSESSING STUDENTS ON THE STANDARDS

• Consider when applying standards and performance indicators with ELs a balanced representation of language proficiency/literacy (reading comprehension and writing skills) and common core/ academic content standards.

• Ensure that the language, literacy, and content standards complement each other.

• Ensure that the instructional targets, standards, and assessments address the different levels of English proficiency/literacy.

• Ensure that the different levels of English proficiency/literacy are progressing systematically throughout a semester.

• Ensure that ELs are presented with and understand the targets and standards they are to achieve on a daily or weekly basis.

• Provide multiple forms and ways of assessing ELs on those targets/ standards.

LT-ELs have experienced multiple ways that schools have failed them. They feel isolated and ostracized. The stigma of "limited English proficient" has been stamped in their hearts as well as their files. They will be apprehensive at best and totally turned off at worst. It will take more than language, literacy, and content to bring them back. They have become experts at reading their teachers' attitudes and dispositions toward them. It will take genuine care and concern from all teachers and school personnel. The relationship a teacher builds with an LT-EL can accelerate the learning. The relationship a principal builds with his teachers can accelerate their learning and renewed commitment to all students.

Oh, and we almost forgot . . . your students will meet core standards, and your school will make AYP.

Questions and Topics for Discussion

1. How do you plan to dispel the myths or clichés that get in the way of successful implementation of effective instructional programs for ELs at your school/district?

2. What structures, support, and services would you incorporate in your theory of action to benefit ELs with carefully crafted and rigorous content instruction?

3. What are the implications from this book for your district, your school, or your classroom?

4. How would you take this book's message to another level to give ELs access to the best education your school/district can offer?

References

Achieve, Inc. (2005). *Rising to the challenge: Are high school graduates prepared for college and work?* Washington, DC: Author.

ACT. (2008). *The forgotten middle: Ensuring that all students are on target for college and career readiness before high school.* Retrieved from http://www.act.org/research/policymakers/pdf/Forgotten MiddleSummary.pdf

Alliance for Excellent Education. (2003). *Adolescents and literacy: Reading for the 21st Century.* Retrieved from http://www.all4ed.org/files/AdolescentsAndLiteracy.pdf

August, D., Goldenberg, C., & Rueda, R. (2010). Restrictive state languagepolicies: Are they scientifically based? In P. Gándara & M. Hopkins (Eds.), *Forbidden language. English learners and restrictive language policies* (pp. 139–158). New York: Teachers College Press.

August, D., & Shanahan, T. (Eds.). (2006). *Developing literacy in second language learners. Report of the National Literacy Panel on Language Minority Children and Youth.* Mahwah, NJ: Lawrence Erlbaum.

August, D., & Shanahan, T. (Eds.). (2008). *Developing reading and writing in second-language learners. Lessons from the report of the National Literacy Panel on Language-Minority Children and Youth.* New York: Routledge.

Balfanz, R., & Legters, N. (2004). *Locating the dropout crisis.* Baltimore: Johns Hopkins University Press.

Barth, R. (1990). *Improving schools from within: Teachers, parents, and principals can make a difference.* San Francisco: Jossey-Bass.

Barth, R. (2006). Improving relationships within the schoolhouse. *Educational Leadership, 63*(6), 8–13.

Batalova, J., & McHugh, M. (2010). *Number and growth of students in US schools in need of English instruction.* Washington, DC: Migration Policy Institute.

Beck, I. L., McKeown, M. G., & Kucan, L. (2002). *Bringing words to life.* New York: Guilford Press.

Beck, I. L., McKeown, M. G., & Kucan, L. (2005). Choosing words to teach. In E. H. Hiebert & M. L. Kamil (Eds.), *Teaching and learning vocabulary* (pp. 207–222). Mahwah, NJ: Lawrence Erlbaum.

Beck, I. L., McKeown, M. G., & Omanson, R. C. (1987). The effects and uses of diverse vocabulary instructional techniques. In M. G. McKeown & M. E. Curtis (Eds.), *The nature of vocabulary acquisition* (pp. 147–163). Hillsdale, NJ: Lawrence Erlbaum.

Beck, I. L., Perfetti, C.A., & McKeown, M. G. (1982). The effects of long-term vocabulary instruction on lexical access and reading comprehension. *Journal of Educational Psychology, 74,* 506–521.

Boyatzis, R. E., & McKee, A. (2005). *Resonant leadership: Renewing yourself and connecting with others through mindfulness, hope, and compassion.* Boston: Harvard Business School Press.

Calderón, M. (1984). *Application of innovation configurations to a trainer of trainers program* (Bilingual Education Selected Papers Series). Los Angeles: Evaluation Dissemination and Assessment Center.

Calderón, M. (1994). Mentoring, peer support, and support systems for first-year minority/bilingual teachers. In R. A. DeVillar, C. J. Faltis, & J. P. Cummins (Eds.), *Cultural diversity in schools: From rhetoric to practice* (pp. 117–141). Albany: University of New York Press.

Calderón, M. (2001). Curricula and methodologies used to teach Spanish-speaking limited English proficient students to read English. In R. E. Slavin & M. Calderón (Eds.), *Effective programs for Latino students* (pp. 251–305). Mahwah, NJ: Lawrence Erlbaum.

Calderón, M. (2007). *Teaching reading to English language learners, grades 6–12: A framework for improving achievement in the content areas.* Thousand Oaks, CA: Corwin.

Calderón, M. (2008a, Jan/Feb). *A retrospective into new paths*. Washington, DC: National Association for Bilingual Education.

Calderón, M. (2008b, December). *Expediting language, literacy and learning for adolescent ELLs*. Santa Clara, CA: California STARlight Consortium.

Calderón, M. (2008c). Teaching academic vocabulary and reading comprehension in grades 6–12. *AccELLerate! The Quarterly Newsletter of the National Clearinghouse for English Language Acquisition, 1*(1), 2–4.

Calderón, M. (2009). Language, literacy and knowledge for ELLs. *Better: Evidence-Based Education, 1*(1), 14–15.

Calderón, M. (in press). *Essentials of teaching reading in K–5th classrooms*. Bloomington, IN: Solution Tree.

Calderón, M., August, D., Slavin, A, Cheung, A., Duran, D., & Madden, N. (2005). Bringing words to life in classrooms with English language learners. In E. H. Hiebert & M. L. Kamil (Eds.), *Teaching and learning vocabulary* (pp. 115–136). Mahwah, NJ: Lawrence Erlbaum.

Calderón, M., & Carreón, A. (1994). Educators and students use cooperative learning to become biliterate and bilingual. *Cooperative Learning, 14*(3), 6–9.

Calderón, M., Carreón, A., Cantú, J., Minaya-Rowe, L. (2008, 2010). *Expediting Comprehension for English Language Learners: Participants' Manual*. New York: Benchmark Education Company.

Calderón, M., & Hertz-Lazarowitz, R. (1994). Implementing cooperative learning in the elementary schools: The facilitator's voice. In S. Sharan (Ed.), *Handbook of cooperative learning methods* (pp. 300–330). New York: Greenwood.

Calderón, M., Hertz-Lazarowitz, R., & Slavin, R. E. (1998). Effects of bilingual cooperative integrated reading and composition on students making the transition from Spanish to English reading. *Elementary School Journal, 99*(2), 153–165.

Calderón, M., Minaya-Rowe, L., Carreón, A., Durán, D., & Fitch, A. (2009a). *Preparing teachers of math, science and social studies with English language learners: A report to the Carnegie Corporation of New York*. New York: Carnegie Corporation of New York.

Calderón, M., Minaya-Rowe, L., Carreón, A., Durán, D., & Fitch, A. (2009b). *Preparing teachers of math, science, social studies and language arts to teach language, literacy and content: A report to the Carnegie Corporation of New York*. New York: Carnegie Corporation of New York.

Calderón, M., & Slavin, R. (2010, May). *Reading and language outcomes of a randomized evaluation of bilingual education programs: What do we mean by quality instruction?* Paper presented to the U.S. Department of Education, Washington, DC.

Calderón, M. E., & Minaya-Rowe, L. (2003). *Designing and implementing two-way bilingual programs: A step-by-step guide for administrators, teachers, and parents*. Thousand Oaks, CA: Corwin.

Carnegie Corporation of New York. (1998). *Turning points: Preparing American youth for the 21st Century*. Retrieved from http://carnegie.org/publications/search-publications/?word=Globalizing+American+Studies+project

Carnegie Council on Advancing Adolescent Literacy. (2010). *Time to act: An agenda for advancing adolescent literacy for college and career success*. New York: Carnegie Corporation of New York.

Center for Public Education. (2008). *Keeping kids in school: What research tells us about preventing dropouts*. Retrieved October 4, 2010, from http://www.centerforpubliced.org/dropouts

Chall, J., & Dale, E. (1995). *Readability revisited*. Cambridge, MA: Brookline.

Collins, J. (2001). *Good to great: Why some companies make the leap and others don't*. New York: HarperBusiness.

Color in Colorado. (May, 2010). *Writing strategies for ELLs*. Retrieved from http://www.colorincolorado.org/educators/teaching/writing_ells

Cummins, J. (1981). The role of primary language development in promoting educational success for language minority students. In California State Department of Education (Ed.), *Schooling and language minority students: A theoretical framework* (pp. 3–50). Los Angeles: California State University.

Cummins, J. (1984). *Bilingualism and special education: Issues in assessment and pedagogy*. Clevedon, England: Multilingual Matters.

Cunningham, A. E. (2005). Vocabulary growth through independent reading and reading aloud to children. In E. H. Hiebert & M. Kamil (Eds.), *Teaching and learning vocabulary: Bringing research to practice* (pp. 45–68). Mahwah, NJ: Lawrence Erlbaum.

Cunningham, A. E., & Stanovich, K. E. (1997). Early reading acquisition and its relation to reading experience and ability 10 years later. *Developmental Psychology, 33*(6), 934–945.

Darling-Hammond, L. (2009). *Teacher quality and student achievement: A review of state policy evidence.* Seattle: University of Washington, Center for the Study of Teaching.

DuFour, R. (2007). In praise of top-down leadership. *School Administrator, 64,* 38–42.

DuFour, R., DuFour, R., Eaker, R., & Karhanek, G. (2010). *Raising the bar and closing the gap: Whatever it takes.* Bloomington, IN: Solution Tree Press.

DuFour, R., & Eaker, R. (1998). *Professional learning communities at work: Best practices for enhancing student achievement.* Alexandria, VA: Association for Supervision and Curriculum Development.

Edmonds, R. (1979). Effective schools for the urban poor. *Educational Leadership, 37*(1), 5–24.

Edmonds, R. (1982). On school improvement: A conversation with Ronald Edmonds. *Educational Leadership, 40*(3), 12–15.

Elmore, R. (2009). *Instructional rounds.* New York: Harvard Educational Press.

Elmore, R. F. (2008). *School reform from the inside out: Policy, practice, and performance.* Cambridge, MA: Harvard Educational Press.

Francis, D. J., Rivera, M. O., Moughamian, A. C., & Lesaux, N. K. (2008). *Effective interventions for reaching reading to English language learners and English language learners with disabilities: Guidance document.* Portsmouth, NH: RMC Research Corporation, Center on Instruction.

Friedman, T. L. (2005). *The world is flat.* New York: Farrar, Straus & Giroux.

Fullan, M. (2001). *Leading in a culture of change.* San Francisco: Jossey-Bass.

Fullan, M. (2008). *Six secrets of change: What the best leaders do to help their organizations survive and thrive.* San Francisco: Jossey-Bass.

Fullan, M. (2010). *Motion leadership.* Thousand Oaks, CA: Corwin.

Genesse, F., Lindholm-Leary, K, Saunders, W., & Christian, D. (2006). *Educating English language learners.* New York: Cambridge University Press.

Gibbons, P. (2002). *Scaffolding language, scaffolding learning. Teaching second language learners in the mainstream classroom.* Portsmouth, NH: Heinemann.

Goldenberg, C. (2008). Teaching English language learners. What the research does—and does not—say. *American Educator, 32*(2), 8–23, 42–44.

Gottlieb, M., Cranley, M. E., & Cammilleri, A. (2007). *The WIDA language proficiency standards and resource guide.* Madison, WI: Board of Regents of the University of Wisconsin System.

Grabe, W. (2009). *Reading in a second language: Moving from theory to practice.* Cambridge, UK: Cambridge University Press.

Graham, S., & Perin, D. (2007). *Writing next. Effective strategies to improve writing of adolescents in middle and high schools.* New York: Carnegie Corporation of New York.

Graves, M. F. (1986). Vocabulary learning and instruction. *Review of Research in Education, 13,* 49–89.

Grossman, P. L., Brown, M., Cohen, J., Loeb, S., Boyd, D., Lanksford, H., & Wyckoff, J. (2009). *Measure for measure: A pilot study linking English language arts instruction and teachers' value-added to student achievement.* Paper presented at the annual meeting of the American Educational Research Association, San Diego, CA.

Guthrie, J. W., & Reed, R. J. (1991). *Educational administration and policy.* Boston: Allyn & Bacon.

Hanushek, E. A. (2004). Our school performance matters. *Journal of Education, 185*(3), 1–6.

Hart, B., & Risley, T. (1995). *Meaningful differences in the everyday lives of young American children.* Baltimore: Brookes.

Hirsh, S. (2006). Consider these critical questions to strengthen your school improvement plan. *Journal of Staff Development, 27,* 59–60.

International Association for the Evaluation of Educational Achievement. (2003). *PIRLS 2001 international report: IEA's study of reading literacy achievement in primary school in 35 countries.* Retrieved from http://timss.bc.edu/pirls2001i/pdf/p1_IR_book.pdf

Jazzar, M., & Algozzine, R. (2005). *Critical issues in educational leadership.* Upper Saddle River, NJ: Allyn & Bacon.

Johnson, D. W, & Johnson, R. T. (1987). *Cooperation and competition: Theory and research.* Edina, MN: Interaction Book Company.

Johnson, D. W, & Johnson, R. T. (1992). *Learning together and alone* (2nd ed.). Englewood Cliffs, NJ: Prentice Hall.

Johnson, P. (2009). The 21st Century skills movement. *Educational Leadership, 67*(1), 11.

Joyce, B., & Showers, B. (1983). *Power in staff development through research in training.* Alexandria, VA: Association for Supervision and Curriculum Development.

Joyce, B., & Showers, B. (2003). *Student achievement through staff development* (3rd ed.). Alexandria, VA: Association for Supervision and Curriculum Development.

Hiebert, E. H., & Kamil, M. L. (Eds.). (2005). *Teaching and learning vocabulary: Bringing research to practice*. Mahwah, NJ: Lawrence Erlbaum.

Kelly, L. K., & Lezotte, L. W. (2003). Developing leadership through the school improvement process. *Journal of School Improvement, 4*, 1–7.

Koretz, D. (2009). How do American students measure up? Making sense of international comparisons. *Future of Children, 19*(1), 37–51.

Lesaux, N. K., Kieffer, M. J., Faller, S. E., & Kelley, J. G. (2010). The effectiveness and ease of implementation of an academic vocabulary intervention for linguistically diverse students in urban middle schools. *Reading Research Quarterly, 45*(2), 196–228.

Liston, D., Borko, H., & Whitcomb, J. (2008). The teacher educator's role in enhancing teacher quality. *Journal of Teacher Education, 59*(2), 111–116. DOI: 10.1177/0022487108215581

Marsh, D., & Calderón, M. (1989). Applying research on effective bilingual instruction in a multi-district inservice teacher training program. *National Association for Bilingual Education Journal, 12*(2), 133–152.

Mashburn, A., Hamre, B., Pianta, R., & Downer, J. (2007, March). *Building a science of classrooms: Three dimensions of child-teacher interactions in PK–3rd grade classrooms*. Paper presented at the biennial meeting of the Society for Research on Child Development, Boston.

McGroarty, M., & Calderón, M. (2005). Cooperative learning for second language learners. In P. A. Richard-Amato & M. A. Snow (Eds.), *Academic success for English language learners* (pp. 174–194). Upper Saddle River, NJ: Pearson Education.

Nagy, W. (2005). Why vocabulary instruction needs to be long-term and comprehensive. In E. H. Hiebert & M. L. Kamil (Eds.), *Teaching and learning vocabulary. Bringing research to practice* (pp. 27–44). Mahwah, NJ: Lawrence Erlbaum.

Nagy, W. E., & Herman, P. A. (1987). Breadth and depth of vocabulary knowledge. Implications for instruction. In M. G. McKeown & M. E. Curtis (Eds.), *The nature of vocabulary acquisition* (pp. 19–35). Hillsdale, NJ: Lawrence Erlbaum.

National Center for Education Statistics. (2007). *The reading literacy of U.S. fourth-grade students in an international context results from the 2001 and 2006 Progress in International Reading Literacy Study (PIRLS)*. Retrieved from http://nces.ed.gov/pubsearch/pubsinfo.asp?pubid=2008017

National Center for Education Statistics. (2009). *Progress in International Reading Literacy Study (PIRLS)*. Retrieved from http://nces.ed.gov/Surveys/PIRLS/

National Center for Learning Disabilities. (2008). *Resources for RTI*. Retrieved from http://www.ncld.org/ld-basics/ld-explained/basic-facts/an-updated-library-of-helpful-resources

National Clearinghouse for English Language Acquisition. (2008). *The growing numbers of English language learners*. Retrieved from http://www.ncela.gwu.edu/files/uploads/9/growingLEP_0708.pdf

National Reading Panel. (2000). *Report of the National Reading Panel: Teaching children to read: An evidence-based assessment of the scientific research literature on reading and its implications for reading instruction* (NIH Publication No. 00–4769). Washington, DC: US Government Printing Office.

National Research Council. (2010). *Preparing teachers: Building evidence for sound policy. Report from the Committee on the Study of Teacher Preparation Programs in the United States*. Washington, DC: The National Academies Press.

Organization for Economic Cooperation and Development. (2003). *First results from PISA 2003: Executive summary*. Retrieved from http://www.oecd.org/dataoecd/1/63/34002454.pdf

Partnership for 21st Century Skills. (2008). *21st Century skills, education, and competitiveness: A resource and policy guide*. Tucson, AZ: Author.

Pianta, R. C., & Hamre, B. K. (2009). Classroom processes and positive youth development: Conceptualizing, measuring, and improving the capacity of interactions between teachers and students. *New Directions for Youth Development, 121*, 33–46.

Pink, D. (2005). *A whole new mind*. New York: Riverhead Books.

RAND Reading Study Group. (2002). *Reading for understanding: Toward a research and development program in reading comprehension*. Retrieved from http://www.rand.org/publications.html

Resnick, L., & Berger, L. (2010). *An American examination system*. Princeton, NJ: Educational Testing Service.

Rotherham, A. J., & Willingham, D. (2009). 21st Century skills: The challenges ahead. *Educational Leadership, 67*(1), 16–21.

Scarcella, R. (2005, December). *Teaching the language of school: How all teachers can support English language learners.* Symposium conducted at the meeting of the Office of English Language Acquisition's Celebrate Our Rising Stars Summit, Washington, DC.

Schlechty, P. (2002). *Working on the work.* San Francisco: Jossey-Bass.

Schmoker, M. (2006). *Results now: How we can achieve unprecedented improvements in teaching and learning.* Alexandria, VA: Association for Supervision and Curriculum Development.

School Leadership for the 21st Century Initiative. (2000). *Leadership for student learning: Reinventing the principalship.* Washington, DC: Institute of Educational Leadership, Inc.

Senechal, M., & Cornell, E. H. (1993). Vocabulary acquisition through shared reading experiences. *Reading Research Quarterly, 28*(4), 361–374.

Sergiovanni, T. J. (2007). *Rethinking leadership: A collection of articles.* Thousand Oaks, CA: Corwin.

Short, D. J., & Fitzsimmons, S. (2007). *Double the work: Challenges and solutions to acquiring language and academic literacy for adolescent English language learners.* Washington, DC: Alliance for Excellent Education.

Silva, E. (2009). Measuring skills for the 21st-century learning. *Phi Delta Kappan, 90*(9), 630–634.

Slavin, R. E. (1975). *Classroom reward structure: Effects on academic performance, social connectedness, and peer norms.* Unpublished doctoral dissertation, Johns Hopkins University, Baltimore.

Slavin, R. E. (1995). *Cooperative learning* (2nd ed.). Boston: Allyn & Bacon.

Slavin, R. E. (1998). Success for All/Exito para Todos: *Effects on the reading achievement of students acquiring English* (Report 19). Baltimore, MD: Johns Hopkins University, Center for Research on the Education of Students Placed at Risk.

Slavin, R. E., & Madden, N. A. (2001). *One million children: Success for all.* Thousand Oaks, CA: Corwin.

Slavin, R. E., Madden, N., Calderón, M., Chamberlain, A., & Hennessy, M. (2010). *Fifth-year reading and language outcomes of a randomized evaluation of transitional bilingual education.* Washington, DC: U.S. Department of Education, Institute for Education Sciences.

Sparks, D. (2009). Status of professional learning. *Learning Forward's multiyear research initiative.* Retrieved October 4, 2010, from http://www.learningforward.org/stateproflearning.cfm

Stahl, S. A., & Fairbanks, M. M. (1986). The effect of vocabulary instruction: A model-based meta-analysis. *Review of Educational Research, 56*(1), 72–110.

Stanovich, K. E. (1986). Mathew effects in reading: Some consequences of individual differences in the acquisition of literacy. *Reading Research Quarterly, 21*, 360-407.

The Common Core Standards. (2010). *Reaching higher: The Common Core Standards validation report.* Retrieved from http://www.corestandards.org/Standards/K12/

The Migration Policy Institute. (2010). *The new demography of U.S. schools.* Retrieved October 4, 2010, from http://www.migrationpolicy.org

The National Commission on Writing. (2005, July). *Writing: A powerful message from state government.* Retrieved from http://www.collegeboard.com/prod_do)wnloads/writingcom/powerful-message-from-state.pdf

Tienda, M. (2007, April). *Latino student demographics.* Paper presented at the conference of the American Educational Research Association, New York.

Tomlinson. C. A. (2008). The goals of differentiation. *Educational Leadership, 66*(3), 26–30.

U. S. Department of Education. (2001). *Outcomes of learning: Results from the 2000 program for international student assessment of 15-year-olds in reading, mathematics, and science literacy* (NCES 2002–115). Retrieved from http://nces.ed.gov/pubs2002/2002115.pdf

U.S. Department of Education. (2007). *Secretary Spellings encourages greater transparency and accountability in higher education at the National Accreditation Meeting.* Retrieved October 4, 2010, from http://www2.ed.gov/news/speeches/2007/12/12182007

U.S. Department of Education, Office of English Language Acquisition. (2008). *Title III of the Elementary and Secondary Education Act of 1965 (ESEA) as Amended by the No Child Left Behind Act of 2001 (NCLB).* Retrieved from http://www2.ed.gov/legislation/FedRegister/other/2008-4/101708a.html

Wright, S. P., Horn, S. P., & Sanders, W. L. (1997). Teacher and classroom context effects on student achievement: Implications for teacher evaluation. *Journal of Personnel Evaluation in Education, 11*(1), 57–67.

Index

CORWIN

A SAGE Company

The Corwin logo—a raven striding across an open book—represents the union of courage and learning. Corwin is committed to improving education for all learners by publishing books and other professional development resources for those serving the field of PreK–12 education. By providing practical, hands-on materials, Corwin continues to carry out the promise of its motto: **"Helping Educators Do Their Work Better."**